Tortugas at 100
Steps in Time & Grace

by
Los Indigenes de Nuestra Señora de Guadalupe
compilation/photography by Pamela Porter
additional images by Jose Luis Nevarez

ISBN: 9780692794074

To request permission to reproduce selections from this book or to order copies, contact EnduringJourneyPress.com

Front cover: Junshiro Molinar and Brittany Pedraza dance with Los Indios at Tortugas Pueblo in 2010.

Back cover: Danzantes Chris Lee and William Martinez dip under the scarves held by two other members (Joe Herrera, right) while repeating the intricate moves of the dance, El Paño, in honor of the Virgin of Guadalupe in 2014. (Photos by Pamela Porter)

Book design by Enduring Journey Press

FOR THE ANCESTORS

CONTENTS

Los Indios, Los Danzantes & Malinches, Capitánes, drummers, and singers commemorate the Pueblo's 100th Anniversary December 12, 2014.

Preface

History lives nearby — just a few miles away, in fact. It's a history born of faith and lovingly passed from one generation to the next, with ritual so ancient that the exact origins are not always identifiable. It throbs with drum beats and chants. It sways with the satiny ribbons adorning dancers who execute steps memorized after watching parents, grandparents, aunts and uncles performing the sequences they learned from those who came before. It resonates with violin and guitar, hymns sung in Spanish, church bells, and it explodes with blasts of shotguns and an abundance of joy during the three-day fiesta devoted to the Virgin of Guadalupe.

This history resides in a New Mexico village known as Tortugas, where Los Indigenes de Nuestra Señora de Guadalupe observed their 100th year of incorporation in 2014; they celebrate their past and anticipate a future that preserves these traditions that meld Catholicism — and the devotion to the Mexican patron saint — and their Native American heritage.

Some of these people moved from El Paso del Norte missions and Isleta del Sur to the Mesilla Valley in the 1880s, and some eventually settled south of Las Cruces in the adjoining villages of San Juan and Guadalupe, called Tortugas.

In order to retain their identity and protect their customs, they incorporated.Families added more adobe homes in the village, and they also began working on community buildings, a cemetery, and a church on property deeded to them. Elders still remember family members who established Los Indigenes de Nuestra Señora de Guadalupe 100 years ago and often share cuentos, or stories, about their ancestors' spirituality and roles in their ancient and newfound

communities. They speak about the rigors of life and discrimination, the strict discipline once connected to the time-honored rituals, respect for the land and its creatures, along with specific incidents, many times miracles granted by La Virgen Morena (dark-skinned Virgin).

I have been privileged to witness and photograph this special place and these people who have allowed my intrusion and welcomed me.

I have learned the three-day fiesta celebrated each December 10-12 is only part of year-long observances and preparation for the sacred processions, prayers, dance, community feast, and pilgrimage to the peak of Tortugas Mountain familiar to those who live in southern New Mexico, West Texas and Juarez, Mexico.

Of course, my inclusion would not be possible without the individuals who introduced me to the Tortugas Pueblo and encouraged me to record this segment of its ongoing history, something that has enriched my soul and will always be a part of my life.

Ethnohistorian Patrick Beckett, known as "Don Patricio" and former all-night cook of an enormous iron pot of albondigas (meat balls) for the feast on December 12, was the first to acquaint me with these customs. His well-researched book, "Tortugas," is co-authored by Terry L. Corbett and serves as an excellent historical overview.

Emma Narvaez, who called the newspaper where I worked years ago, was my second link. "Do you want to know the real story of Tortugas?" her sweet, frail voice asked.

Of course I did! I visited her home several times, and she shared her long heritage with me in bits and pieces and also was an ally when I first asked permission to photograph Tortugas for an art project at New Mexico State University 20+ years ago.

Emma's daughters, especially Philly and husband John Dickson, have supported my efforts and also fought to retain Pueblo access to a peaceful Tortugas Mountain, which Dominic Fierro, La Corporación's president in 2012-15, continues to do.

After 100 years, uninformed zoning threatens to surround the mountain with noisy roadways and businesses, and gaining access to their sacred peak is becoming increasingly difficult.

Emma's son, Henry, served as Cacique (spiritual leader) for the Pueblo until April 6, 2015, when he nominated his son, Patrick, to succeed him. Patrick had been serving as his Ayudante (helper) for several years, absorbing knowledge from the Cacique for the future.

The Corporation's Board of Directors will determine the next Cacique, after receiving input from Pueblo members.

"You have just witnessed history!" Dominic Fierro tells me after the emotion-filled resignation from a life-long position was delivered during a meeting.

And so the history continues, to be added to the extensive documents and photos collected by Pablo Fierro, keeper of the Pueblo's past. He and his wife, Marciala, and children David and wife Sylvia Fierro, and Patsy and her husband, Frank Torres, have shared their memories.

Miguel Parra and his relatives have included and educated me as well. Special thanks also to Felipe Chavez and his gracious wife, Katie, who believed in this project from day one. Lupe Dominguez Flores, and her late husband, Daniel, were others always willing to help.

Dear friends Fermina Paz and Carolina Carabajal, Pueblo potters, and all of their extended family members, especially Fermina's late husband, Frank (Kiko), along with Margie Lazos, Sonia Lazos and Michael Molinar (and his parents Reymundo and Dolores), Sylvia Lozano, Rafael (Buddy) and Kathy Paz, humble me with their kindness and gifts.

Without the help of talented poet and writer Rosemary Estrada Kirby and also Corporation book committee members Arianna Fierro, Jeanette Castillo, and Dominic Fierro, this story could not be told.

Credit for the text and caption information within these pages goes to the many people who have contributed their perspective for this book; I am honored to record and assemble these cuentos.

Tortugas photographer buddy Jose Luis Nevarez has always shared his knowledge of events; he has also generously provided several engaging images, which are credited, for this offering.

I gained further insight from both the Danza Chichimeca Azteca and Danza Guadalupana Azteca membes. Many thanks!

Mayordomos as well as the Capitánes, the men chosen to protect and oversee these traditions, deserve recognition as well. I hope they are respectfully represented in this endeavor. Parish priests and both Bishops of the Las Cruces Diocese have been tolerant and helpful.

Dancers, musicians, cooks, servers, and dishwashers are equally important in honoring their heritage. To those I have failed to mention, please accept my apologies.

And to the soft-spoken man who once appeared before me in La Casa de Comida and reassured, "The Virgin will help you!" when I expressed doubts over the enormity of this project: She certainly has.

Gracias a todos. ¡Viva Guadalupe!

– Pamela Porter, 2014

Welcome to Tortugas, New Mexico!
... home of Los Indigenes de Nuestra Senora de Guadalupe, the Tortugas Pueblo, and the Shrine & Parish of Our Lady of Guadalupe

As time passes, things change. Some of the changes are extremely significant, while others are important and others are small yet necessary. This is true for every civilization, country, state, community and organization. The core reason for most changes, regardless of size, is to learn, adapt, and adjust. Changes within Los Indigenes de Nuestra Señora de Guadalupe (La Corporación) are no different.

For over 150 years, our ancestors endured many changes. From constant moving due to revolts, or the European settlements, or finding places that allowed us to dance and worship, change was evident.

In the early 1900s, with the help of Colonel Eugene Van Patten, an agreement was made between the elders of La Corporación and the Village of San Juan de Dios. The agreement was simple...build a Roman Catholic Church for the Village of San Juan de Dios and La Corporación members would be allowed to move just south of the Village. Forty acres of land were granted to the Village of Guadalupe (just south of the Village of San Juan de Dios) by the Doña Ana Bend Board of Commissioners in 1908. These two villages are commonly referred to as Tortugas. Construction on the church began shortly thereafter.

There were always people who doubted that we would survive and continue with our customs and traditions beyond a couple of decades, if that. Colonel Van Patten and the Board of Commissioners wanted to ensure the Pueblo would continue. Thus, they took action.

Shortly after New Mexico became a state in the United States of America, Colonel Van Patten and the Board of Commissioners of the Village of Guadalupe created a non-profit corporation to ensure that what they built would remain for many, many years. From generation to generation, we have to give thanks to our prior generations. They understood the key to continuing our customs and traditions was to teach the younger generations.

If our ancestors didn't pass down the customs and traditions, we would not be where we are today. As a fourth-generation member of La Corporación, I truly believe this. Over the last one hundred years, it hasn't always been easy.

Growth of Las Cruces has completely surrounded Tortugas. While technology and also commercialization continue to grow and advance civilization, we have continued to incorporate some of these advances, while still maintaining our customs and traditions as we were taught by our ancestors.

As we celebrate our centennial anniversary of incorporation, we have to be ever mindful of our past while preparing for the future.

Over the last few years, La Corporación has adopted a motto, "Preserving Our Past...Ensuring Our Future." This continues to be an emphasis and the key for La Corporación for future generations.

As President, I am ever mindful of all of those people who "sat in the chair" prior to me and how I can continue what they started while preparing La Corporación for the future. How do we continue to be a part of the surrounding community while remaining vigilant with the various activities that surround La Corporación and Tortugas? It is a balancing act that has to be performed and isn't necessarily easy. I, like my predecessors, rely on the elders to provide wisdom, guidance and our history.

One of the things La Corporación is very mindful of is the continuous teaching of our customs and traditions to the next generation of Tortugeños. The key to our continued existence is the youth. Between the current mediums of social media and extracurricular school activities, there is a constant struggle to keep the youth involved in learning our customs and traditions. I hope and pray that our inclusion of various aspects of social media, while keeping with our customs and traditions, keep the young people engaged.

On behalf of the Board of Directors, the Centennial Book Committee, as well as the membership, and all of those who have or currently are a part of La Corporación, I hope you enjoy what you read, see and learn in this book.

Photo by Jose Luis Nevarez

La Corporación President Dominic Fierro addresses the celebrants on December 12 during the 2014 Fiesta.

For some, this book will provide a glimpse of who we are, what we do and what we believe in. For others, it will bring back memories of time long forgotten, while for others it provides an opportunity to show their family, friends and acquaintances a place where they may have visited and were a part of our annual three-day December fiesta.

May Our Lady of Guadalupe and her son, Jesus Christ, continue to watch over and bless all Tortugeños, near and far, and all past, present and future generations.

¡Viva Tortugas!

— Dominic Fierro, President
2012-2015

Tortugas Pueblo is a product of different cultures and religious beliefs

Members of Tortugas Pueblo, located south of Las Cruces, New Mexico, include descendants of the Tiwa and Piro tribes who inhabited the Rio Grande Valley from Isleta Pueblo south to present-day Socorro, New Mexico, and east to Gran Quivera.

Many of these indigenous Native Americans traveled south with the Spanish from northern New Mexico as they relocated to the area of El Paso del Norte (El Paso, Texas), during the Pueblo Revolt of 1680.

When the Spanish returned to northern New Mexico in 1692, many of these people — including the descendants living in Tortugas Pueblo — remained in the south.

The Tiwas and Piros have combined their beliefs into a single religion, and they jointly perform rituals for the spirits of the wind, sun, sky, and earth. They teach their children the various myths which their ancestors carried south with them in 1680.

Beginning in 1580, the Spanish introduced the Catholic religion to the Native American peoples of New Mexico, including the ancestors of Tortugas Pueblo.

The Catholic priests adhered to the doctrine that the Catholic religion was the only true way to salvation. Accordingly, the Pueblo was forced to practice its form of religion in the secrecy of the kivas.

To this day, Tortugas Pueblo struggles with notions of fundamentalism on both sides — Native American and Catholicism.

Both sides have their strong supporters, who want to return to a more rigid adherence to the practices of their respective beliefs.

The religious celebrations and customs of Tortugas Pueblo truly are a blend of Native American beliefs and Catholic religion.

For example, the drum is played and dances are carried out in traditional Native American costumes. However, the major feast day is on the day assigned to the Pueblo by the Catholic priests.

The dances are carried out in front of the Catholic church and the dancers then go inside to mass; however, the ceremonial drum remains outside the church to show a degree of independence from the Catholic church.

Tortugas Pueblo has managed to accommodate the religious beliefs of the Tiwas, Piros, and Catholic priests.

If history is any indicator, it is likely that Tortugas Pueblo will continue to find ways to accommodate the religious beliefs of the various members, regardless of tribal ancestry or branch of Christianity, while preserving its Native American traditions.

— an overview of Tortugas Pueblo by Henry and Patrick Narvaez

Humero (keeper of the smoke), Reymundo Molinar, instructs a young participant on the proper way to place creosote – "waymi" – on a flameless fire that blesses participants in the Cerco.

La Corporación de Los Indigenes de Nuestra Señora de Guadalupe Turns 100

"I kind of hate to call it the Corporation - it's not THAT type of a corporation," says Michael Molinar, a member of Los Indios who has served as Capitán de la Guerra and is also a member of Los Indigenes. "I prefer to refer to it — and this place — as the Pueblo. We'd be people without a home if we didn't have that 40 acres granted the Corporation. It's the vehicle that moves everything," he observes.

"It is different than a normal corporation — well, we have bylaws and all that, but I think that the intent was to protect the assets of the Pueblo," explains David Fierro, who also danced and drummed with Los Indios and has served as a Mayordomo and Capitán more than once. "We owe a lot to Col. Van Patten; I guess we're just lucky that he married a Native girl (Benita Madrid Vargas, of Piro descent)."

Col. Eugene Van Patten is held in high regard by everyone, it seems. He spearheaded efforts to apply for the 40 acres from the Doña Ana Bend Colony Land Grant and created the legal entity that was able to secure that land in 1908. "He was a rare soul. He had a big heart," Molinar says.

A quiet ceremony on April 26, 2014 marked the Pueblo's centennial. Pueblo officials and members of Los Indios and Los Danzantes commemorated the event with a procession to the church, dances, and a mass. In the photo above are Patrick Narvaez, Reymundo Molinar, and Henry Narvaez, second row: Lawrence Jimenez, Christine Misquez, Bill Acosta, and Libby Valles; last row: Joe Raymond Fierro and Martín Barela.

Capitánes (facing page) for 2014 include (from left) Arturo Montoya, Miguel Parra, Capitán de la Guerra Ed Fierro, Frank Narvaez, and Felipe Chavez.

"Our ancestors were very insightful in how the Corporation is set up; there is a distribution of power and responsibility," maintains David Fierro. He traces a triangle with his finger, and at each point he names the people who oversee its operation, saying, "It's a three-legged stool, with the Mayordomos in charge of the Fiesta, the five Capitánes in charge of ceremony, and the Board of Directors takes care of all of the administrative part of the operation."

Two people of great importance also contribute to the Pueblo's operation: the Capitán de la Guerra (first war captain) and the Cacique, spiritual leader.

According to Joe Raymond Fierro, Monarca Assistant, former Capitán, and member of Los Indígenes de Nuestra Señora de Guadalupe: "The Capitán de la Guerra is the person with the highest authority in our Corporation. If there is a conflict, he's the one who has the authority to settle it."

Capitánes from the previous year generally select one Pueblo member to join them as Quinto Capitán, then the fifth Capitán moves into the forth position and "on up the line," Joe Raymond says.

"We work all year for three days — we're here to serve the Pueblo," Molinar points out, referring to what he calls "Día Doce," or the December 10-12 Feast of Our Lady of Guadalupe. "We start in earnest in October. It's not a matter of who's going to do what — everybody has a job," he says. "That means everything from cleaning toilets to cleaning the Pueblo grounds and the mountain." The Capitán de la Guerra coordinates those efforts and often works round the clock.

"We don't even see Mike for long periods of time; the family definitely plays second fiddle," says Sonia Lazos, whose roots also stretch back to the Pueblo beginnings. "But we understand and help all we can,"

she says of herself and their two children.

The Cacique's position follows bloodlines, with Felipe Roybal being named the first in the late 1800s. He was followed by Vicente Roybal, then Ernesto Domiguez until his death.

More than 100 years later, Henry Narvaez serves in the position his great-grandfather initially held and continues to carry out the Native American rituals he learned from his "Tio Neto," mother Emma and aunt Chepa, Josefa Salcido.

Narvaez recalls learning the chants and drumming from his relatives, even singing the Tiwa songs while washing dishes together as a family. Although he currently lives in Albuquerque, he's passing his heritage along to his children and grandchildren.

The Cacique is present for all events, along with his son Patrick. "One of the symbols is the new moon and the star on the tombe; there is a place that has that symbol and the sipapu — that's where they go to make the Cacique. That's where I will go to take Patrick," Henry says.

For years, there was no Cacique, but Pedro Pedraza performed the duties and then Ernesto Dominguez stepped in. Pablo Fierro served as "Cacique Interino" (acting Cacique) until Narvaez assumed the position.

"Ernesto was very religious," Pablo remembers. "He choreographed one of the dances — number four — where they (Los Indios dancers) turn in the four directions. I first danced in 1938," he says. Pablo has retained files, newspaper clippings, minutes from early meetings, and old photos to be placed in the planned Pueblo community center, La Escuelita.

"All those papers — they were Ernesto's," David reminds his dad, who nods in agreement. "Your compadre wanted you to have them."

"April 12, 1914, is the date of our incorporation, so this is a special day.

"We danced 100 years ago for the Bishop at the train depot in Las Cruces. He said, 'It's too bad the tradition won't last.' Through the years we have had our ups and downs, and we don't always see eye to eye; our faith keeps us together."

— address, 100th Anniversary by Ed Fierro, Capitán de la Guerra 2014

Katie and Felipe Chavez have been involved as Mayordomos and officers in the Corporation for many years. Felipe has also served as a Capitán. He says, "In order to become a member, you have to be sponsored by an active member." Katie adds, "And you have to show an interest — that you will be here during the Fiesta and you know about the traditions. You have to already be a little bit involved."

Each applicant appears before the membership during one of the monthly Corporation meetings, are introduced by their sponsor and ask to join, making a brief presentation about why they wish to become part of the Pueblo. Their six-month probation follows.

All share a fierce desire to continue the Corporation's mission of protecting what early members initiated. Most realize that change is inevitable, but still wish to follow the traditional path.

Joe Raymond Fierro was amazed at the disarray of land holdings and deeds of the original 40 acres when he began researching the property as part of his "Ensure Our Future" campaign.

"The Corporation had 11 different properties listed with the county in different names," he says while shaking his head. "We're trying to identify what is ours and what is not ours." The committee he heads also sponsors fundraisers to pay property taxes and promote the Pueblo.

"The fiesta is not going to die during my generation's watch!" vows Joe Raymond.

Felipe Chavez states, "As president, I tried to keep the customs that were passed down by those who were here before us. But these traditions will not last exactly as they are now."

Michael Molinar agrees. "Whether or not the Fiesta keeps the same form, I think it will continue — there are lots of people who want to help. But it depends on the younger generation," he says, casting a glance at his son, Junshiro, and daughter, Iashire, who feel the weight of their responsibilities at only 17 and 12.

"I plan do that, and I'm learning," Junshiro says, "but I hope you guys figure it all out and get it written down for us."

"If my granddaughter could experience even 80 percent of what I have had, that would be wonderful," David Fierro reflects. "As an analogy - it's a car, a Model "A" right now. In 100 years, it will still be a car, but it will have a lot of different gadgets. The biggest challenge is keeping the core customs and traditions of the Pueblo intact."

Ethany Fierro carries the water that Rev. Vincent Peterson, O.F.M. Conv., dips a branch of creosote in to bless the congregation during Mass.

Sanctuario de Nuestra Señora de Guadalupe
observes Centennial in 2014

Parishioners and Tortugas Pueblo members, along with all four of the dance groups, gathered for an outdoor mass that recognized the present church's beginnings. A chapel built on the site in 1910 was enlarged after the property was transferred to the Diocese of Tucson in 1914. Its side brick tower was too heavy for the adobe walls, but many say the priest at the time did not approve of the Pueblo Mission architecture and had it removed. A number of San Juan residents helped design and reconstruct the central steeple in 1968.

In photo above, Most Rev. Oscar Cantú, S.T.D.D.D., and Bishop, with most Rev. Ricardo Ramirez, Bishop Emeritus of the Roman Catholic Dioccese of Las Cruces, walk with Mayordomos J.R. and Rosie Stewart, Lawrence Jimenez and Christine Misquez, and Libby Valles and Bill Acosta at right.

Los Indigenes assume positions of responsibility to protect traditions

Capitánes (from left) Arturo Montoya and Michael Molinar, along with Cacique Henry Narvaez and Ayudante Patrick Narvaez join Mayordomos Bertha and Raymond Tellez as they escort the sacred image in 2011.

Capitán John Levesque paints the face of community member Martha Lozano after placing the tradition three dots on the cheeks and chin on her baby as Pueblo dancers prepare for the observation of San Juan's Day at Tortugas Pueblo. Men are painted with lines on either side of the nose, as tradition dictates.

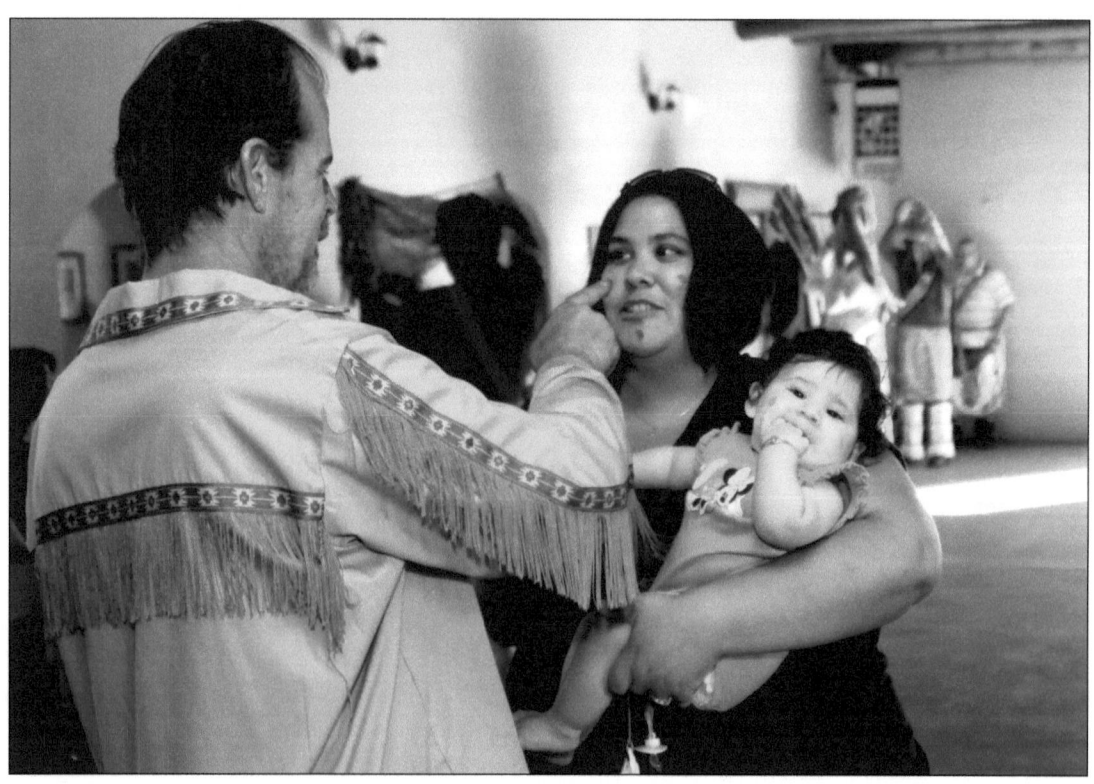

Monarca Ernesto Misquez (right), during a 1989 celebration, leads Los Danzantes members in matachine dances in front of the church. At left is Frank Marta.

Below, Corporation members and officials teach Tiwa drumming and chants in 2003 to boys who will carry on the traditions of their fathers and grandfathers. Pictured from left are Francisco Rayos, Arturo Montoya, Michael Molinar, Tony Parra, Johnny Hernandez, Miguel Parra, Phillip Paz, and Reymundo Molinar.

"They know about us up north at Isleta Pueblo. We're known as 'Ba-Kora-Tiue': the Turtle Pueblo."
— Michael Molinar

Pueblo Dancers, Los Indios, retain Native American rituals

Photo by Jose Luis Nevarez

Cacique Henry Narvaez and Capitán de la Guerra Michael Molinar address the Pueblo dancers and Capitánes after the 2013 return of the Virgen de Guadalupe's image to the Capilla on January 1.

In a Tortugas home that once served as the meeting house for the community, descendants of Maria de la Luz Duran, a Tigua Indian, and Faustino Pedraza, a Piro, pick each other's brains for details from their past. They recall that this was the first house in the newly created village of Guadalupe right after the Corporación Los Indígenes de Nuestra Señora de Guadalupe was granted a 40-acre tract of land.

December 11th's pilgrimage to Tortugas Mountain began and ended at the "little jacalito" that has grown over the years, and the Baile de Olla was also held there. "We even found 100-year-old confetti in the walls here," says Margie Lazos.

Carolina Carabajal shares that native people, many from the Tigua Pueblo in El Paso, were headed "home" in the late 19th Century to reunite with their Isleta Pueblo relatives after their long exile following the Pueblo Revolt of 1680.

Records show that they made it as far as the Ft. Fillmore/Las Cruces area, where they met Indians from the Guadalupe Mission and Mexican Pueblo of Senecu.

Others say the migration was caused by overcrowding of the Pueblos around Paso del Norte, and when southern New Mexico opened up for settlement, people came in search of work.

"My mom taught us a little bit of the language, not sentences, but a few of the words — 'eagle feather, nonIndian, let's go.' Mr. Gonzales, one of the old-timers, he would tell us what the songs were about, like 'let's be one tribe and not fight anymore.'" — Fermina Paz

"We weren't taught the language because, I was told, that the grown-ups didn't want us to know what they were saying. It's sad that we've lost it. - Margie Lazos

"I'm trying to teach myself. But it's tricky because the language is a combination of Tiwa and Piro; I'm slowly starting to get it." - Bianca Paz

Lorena Torres-Martinez and Francisco Rayos dance with Los Indios in 2012. They are accompanied by (back, from center) Rosie Stewart, and Sally Hernandez.

Los Indios dancers Rebecca Torres and Lorenzo Rios (above) honor the Virgin of Guadalupe in 2006.

After the 2004 Fiesta, Margie Lazos offers encouragement as her young granddaughter Iashire dances behind her father, Michael Molinar, in La Casa del Pueblo.

Capitán Reymundo Molinar, leads Francis Wood durng a San Juan Feast Day dance in June of 2010 (facing page).

Ethnohistorian Pat Beckett writes that a group named "Los Inditos de Las Cruces" materialized from these origins, bringing with them the customs passed down from Pueblo ancestors.

The dances and chants, sung to the beat of the original Tortugas drum, reflect that heritage. Twelve males, each carrying the guaje or gourd rattle, and twelve female dancers recreate the deliberate, measured steps to at least a dozen or more remembered chants, which are specific for each dance.

For most participants, this is the way they honor their promesa made to the patroness –La Virgen Morena (the Dark Virgin).

The men and boys (bailadoros) are dressed in trajes, which are constructed from tan material and red fringe, many of them made by Katie Chavez, who has sewn more of the ceremonial garments throughout the years than she can count. The men grasp hand-made bows called arcos and dance with high steps and their heads bent in reverence.

The women and girls, the bailadoras, hold feathered arrows that sparkle in the sunlight as they move them in unison or dance with male partners. They wear a single-shouldered black dress called a manta that is edged in decorative trim and belted at the waist. Multicolored ribbons, whose colors hold special meaning, and a veil flutter down their backs from a headband.

Photos from the 1880s show the Pueblo dancers, dressed in similar clothing, dancing in front of the now-demolished St. Genevieve's Catholic Church in the heart of Las Cruces. During an interview before her death, Emma Narvaez clearly remembers her family talking about those days before the incorporation and transition to the community of Guadalupe.

"The feast used to take place at 343 E. Amador," she recalls. And the pilgrimage "where they would make their altar" was to a pear orchard in the Mesilla Valley.

A group of five men, the Capitánes, serve as the ceremonial officials for these dancers and the Fiesta. They hold staffs woven from native tree branches that were removed by hand, as custom dictates that no metal object can be used when gathering these varas.

They carry their special staffs as a symbol of their authority and are strict when certain rules are violated or someone is disrespectful during any of the ceremonies. "When I used to come with my dad (Leonardo Crispín), you could not walk in front of the Capitánes because they had the varas — and they would whip our legs! Nowadays they can't do that; it's considered abuse," offers Katie Chavez, who learned how to behave the painful way, a common experience for many of the older members.

"The three days of the Fiesta in December are special to me. Everything is done with such dedication and humility. For those three days if you allow yourself, as I do, you can lose yourself in the moment. For those days, emotionally and spiritually, the rest of the world does not exist. It's humbling," concludes Los Indios bailadora Jeannette Castillo.

Los Danzantes have Matachine roots from Mexico and Spain

Just as there is a visual record of Los Indios dancing on the grounds of St. Genevieve's Catholic Church, old photos show Tortugas Pueblo's other dancers, Los Danzantes, were also thriving at the turn of the century. They honored the Virgin at the former Las Cruces landmark in the heart of town.

This type of dance, the Matachine, takes several forms, but is unique in that it is performed in both Hispanic villages and Indian Pueblos throughout the Southwest and Mexico.

An aura of mystery surrounds the Los Danzantes, who wear imposing cupiles, or headpieces decorated with bits of mirrors, jewels, and images of La Virgen de Guadalupe. Fringe covers their eyes and scarves conceal faces, while colorful satin ribbons trail from the back of the cupiles past their knees. All wear an altár (apron-like scarf) with the Virgin's image on it.

A red sash over the shoulder signifies the side on which the man dances, while Malinches wear a blue sash across their right shoulder so that it never covers their heart, explains Lawrence Jimenez, who danced with the group many years before serving as Mayordomo with his wife, Christine Misquez, in 2013 and 2014.

"Our dance is from Spanish origins with lots of Native American influences mixed in," he says, pointing out that "soldiering" or forming files (lines) is an indigenous characteristic, as is shaking the gourd rattle (guaje).

"The dress reflects Spanish Catholicism, with the glittering palma representing the Father, Son, and Holy Ghost and is carried in the other hand. Frilly leggings, called chaparones or polainas, cover the lower legs for the purpose of scaring snakes away with each stamp of the foot. "So, I guess we have St. Patrick to thank for that," Jimenez smiles.

No drums accompany Los Danzantes, but a sole musician plays the sonas (tunes) on violin for the dances.

Currently, violinist Leo Perez provides the music, but he worries that there are no younger violinists to take his place, especially since he has moved to Houston and commutes to Tortugas for each celebration.

Although this traditional music has been transcribed and it sounds like simple, repetitive tunes to the untrained ear, he points out, "That doesn't mean others can easily play it." There are subtleties in the rhythm that are difficult to reproduce, explains Perez, who has been playing for the Danzantes since he was a teen.

Malinches, young girls dressed in white who accompany the male dancers, represent the spirit of purity, and they take turns dancing with the group of men.

Gabby Fierro says, "I have danced with the Danzantes for two years and loved every minute of it. I enjoyed learning the dances and even teaching my little cousin the moves for each dance. My favorite dance is the Paño dance (scarf dance). I've been warned that if I get any taller, I may not be able to dance next year, which I'm hoping doesn't happen," she blushes.

The fringe on Miguel Silva's distinctive cupil sways in rhythm to the violin as he dances.

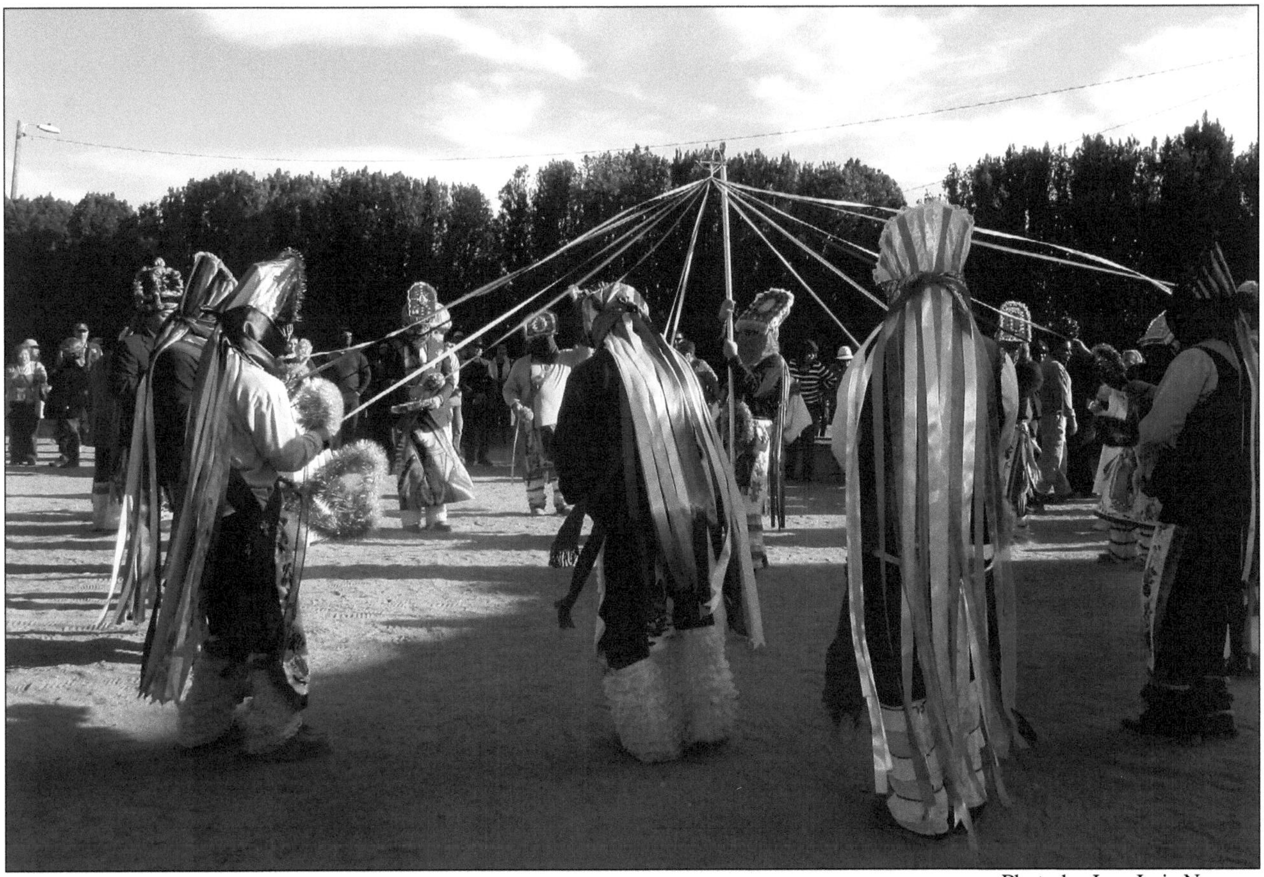

Photo by Jose Luis Nevarez

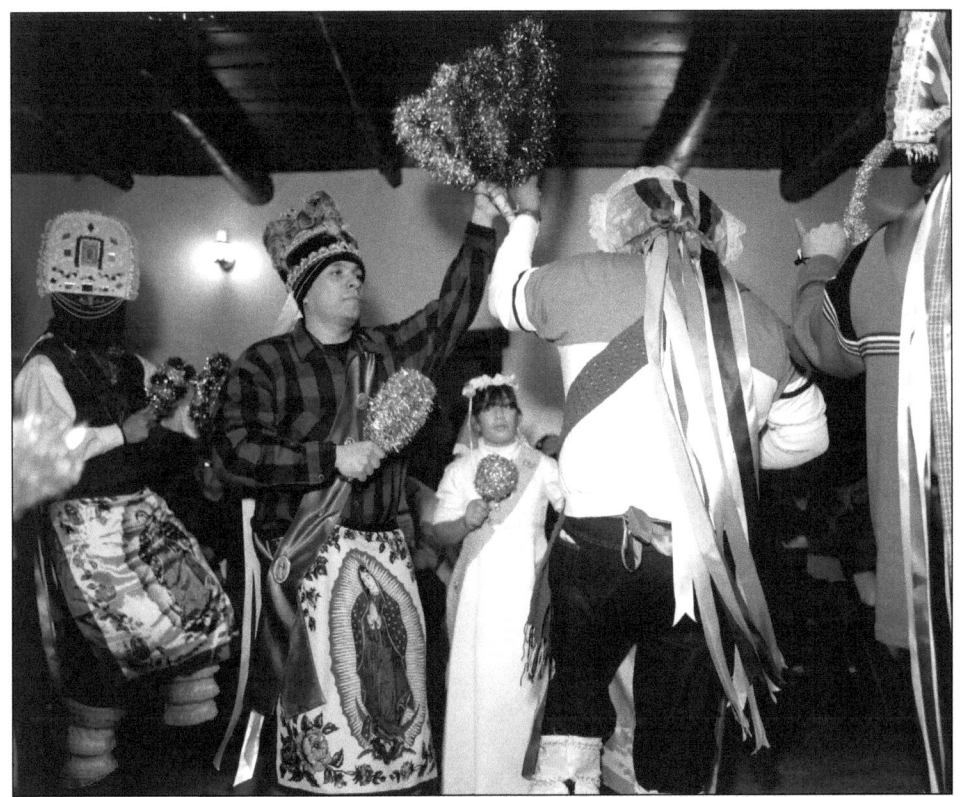

Danzantes wrap a maypole with ribbons by weaving around it in an intricate repetition of steps (top).

Monarca Assistant Milo Reyes, leads the traditional steps on January 1 in La Casa del Pueblo (left).

"Our dance is a prayer to the Virgin," shares Joe Raymond Fierro, who danced a few years with Los Indios before settling in with Los Danzantes.

"There also tends to be a more religious focus." Fierro serves as assistant Monarca with Milo Reyes, and the two often take turns with overseeing the 12 dances performed during the Fiesta and on January 1 with Monarca Martín Barela.

"I'm in charge of the dancers," Barela says, "but I am also supposed to help with all Pueblo functions behind the scenes." Instead of the cupil and scarf, he and his assistants share a shimmering crown topped with a cross. He was drawn to this group because he liked the anonymity it provided. Ironically, the Monarca and his assistants do not cover their faces.

He smiles and says, "After I married Susie (Carabajal), her family broke me out of my shell." They also helped him learn the steps he will repeat for a lifetime of devotion to the Virgin of Guadalupe and Pueblo customs.

Born in 1909, Emma Narvaez said her earliest memory is dancing as a Malinche by 6 or 7 years old. "The Matachine dance did come from Juarez," she said. "And my father learned from the first Monarca. Then, when I got older I went to the Indian dances." Female dancers throughout the years have a shared history of participating as children in this group and dancing with Los Indios as women.

"If you want to know the true meaning of the Fiesta, join the Danzantes for a year," Fierro recommends.

Monarca Martín Barela and Eric Fierro (to the right on the facing page) join Danzante members during the 100th year celebration in Tortugas.

Above, cupiles adorned with images of the Virgin of Guadalupe are placed on a table in La Casa de Comida while their owners take a break to eat.

"January is an important month because it's a time of transitions...

"And standing on the outside, looking in, you can see the new people — Capitánes, Board of Director members, Mayordomos – coming in with new ideas and people stepping down. Tortugas has a way of making people grow. And you walk away as a different person.

"I think January starts that. It makes us have to do things together. Then things slow down in the summer, and they pick up again. It's constantly growing and evolving. It's a circle of life."

— Patrick Narvaez

Tortugas Pueblo's Los Indios dancers Michael Molinar and his mother, Dolores Molinar, honor tradition by performing dances passed down by Tiwa ancestors for the Virgin of Guadalupe January 1, 1993. Bailadoras Sylvia Lozano and Carmen Orta are also pictured.

The Virgin's image takes a place of honor in the Sanctuario December 11 – January 1. The palanquin, which is decorated differently each year by current Mayordoros, is escorted in a procession January 1 to the small chapel, La Capilla, where She resides until December 10.

Malinches, young girls dressed in white who dance with Los Danzantes, enter the Sanctuario de Nuestra Señora de Guadalupe in 2013 for a Mass that is part of January 1 ceremonies, which conclude when the image of the Virgin is returned to La Capilla during a procession. Malinches pictured from right are Marrissa Padilla, Gabriella Fierro, and Ethany Fierro.

Mayordomos Ray Hernandez and Robert Parra remove the Virgin's palanquin for the 2004 procession to return it to the Capilla.

"The glue that holds us together is our faith. We all look to Our Lady of Guadalupe – we have a great devotion to Her."

— Ed Fierro, Capitán de la Guerra 2014

During a packed Mass on December 12, 1996, dance groups, Fiesta officials and the public receive Holy Communion from Las Cruces Bishop Ricardo Ramirez. From center Danzante to left are Joe Reymond Fierro, Isidro Fierro, Malinche Lisa Cano, and Mayordomo Fred Salas.

"Have you noticed that the Vigen de Guadalupe, our Holy Mother Mary, has one leg bent? She dances with you!"

— Bishop Ricardo Ramirez

"And Her hands ... are they clasped in prayer, or does She clap in delight?"

— Rev. Vincent Peterson

"Indian Girl Dancing"

Photo by Jose Luis Nevarez

Isis Kirby Spitzig, 3, learns to dance at the Tortugas Pueblo during the 2012 Fiesta.

With downward gaze,
her arms move gracefully,
shifting the breeze through which she moves,
her feet dancing softly on sacred ground.

Mother and Abuela on either side,
she glances frequently at their feet,
emulating their movements.

Her arms have always known the tombé's beat,
the heartbeat she has heard and felt
since before her birth.

She wants to follow the chanters and the tombé
but two gentle words and a soft touch on her shoulder
guide her back into the Circle.

She is only three now, her form very small
amid the generations of dancers:
Her spirit, her heart, her love, her innocent faith,
however, fill her body
and will continue to grow as she grows
into the danza.

The spirits of the ancestors
dance alongside her,
smiling, pleased, honored
by this Indian girl dancing.
— Rosemary Estrada Kirby

"Being part of this Pueblo as a dancer, a member, a Mayordoma has changed me for the better. I am a better person because of this Pueblo, and I love it. My only hope is that my daughter and my nieces experience and continue these great traditions that we have here."
- Arianna Fierro

"When I put on my manta (traditional dress for Los Indios bailadoras), I feel like a different person. I am proud to be part of this tradition; I am honored to dance for the Virgin."
- Jeannette Castillo

Monarca Peter Ferrales and violinist Leo Perez join Los Danzantes in front of the Sanctuario de Nuestra Señora de Guadalupe in their moving form of prayer to the Virgin, January 1, 2009.

The ornate cupiles of two Danzante members catch the last rays of light during the January celebration.

Marley Morales (right), Sylvia Paz, and other bailadoras of Los Indios dance in front of the church before going in to pray in 2013.

They are joined by Los Danzantes and the other two participating dance groups, Danza Guadalupana Azteca (right) and Danza Azteca Chichimeca (top, facing page). All dancers participate during the afternoon and also the early evening procession that returns the image of Our Lady of Guadalupe to La Capilla, where She resides until December 10 of the following year.

Bailadora Sally Hernandez receives a blessing from Patrick Narvaez, who uses smoke from the traditional cigarillo made from cornhusks and tobacco, facing page.

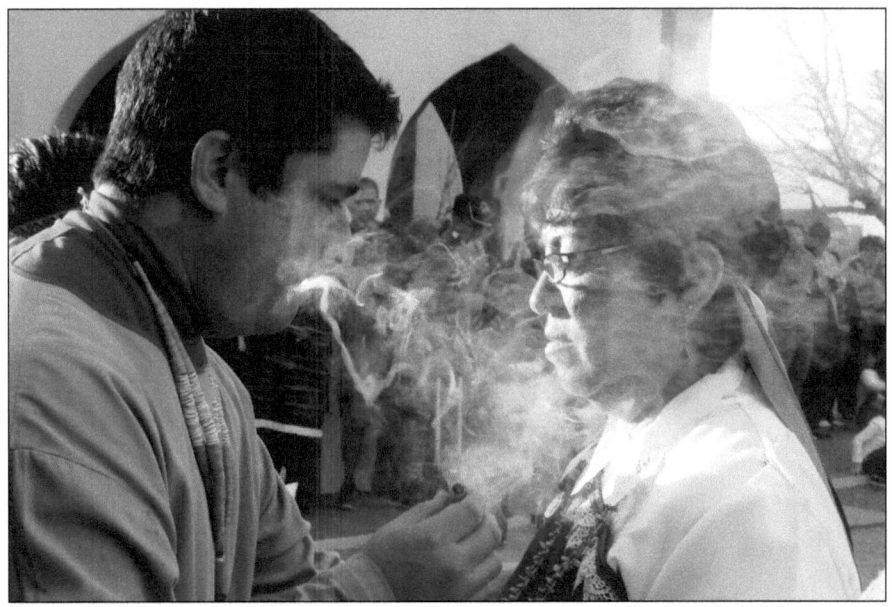

← *Tortugas at 100* —

Female members of Los Indios dance while escorting the revered palanguin through the streets of Tortugas, top left.

Mayordomos Rosalie and Margarito Fierro, left, and David and Sylvia Fierro, along with Fiesta participants, accompany the image to her resting place, La Capilla, during the 1990s.

Capitán de la Guerra (First War Captain) Ed Fierro watches over the Los Indios bailadoras Brittany Pedraza, Jeannette Castillo, and others as they enter La Capilla to bid farewell to the Virgin of Guadalupe's image January 1.

Tortugas at 100

"I danced for the Virgin, with Los Danzantes, for 30 years. I used to smoke, and I quit dancing for a while because I got out of breath. But in 1970, when I was out of work, I promised Our Lady to dance once more and asked for help. Within 30 days I was hired. I quit smoking, and I danced for many more years in Her honor. It's been a good life."
– Antonio Marta

The faithful pay homage to the Virgin of Guadalupe after returning the decorated image to La Capilla after the January 1 procession. A choir, accompanied by guitar, sings as Mayordomo John Levesque and the faithful pray (at left).

Above, Young boys are dwarfed by Los Danzantes members Martín Barela, left, and Joe Raymond Fierro, right, visiting La Capilla in 2004.

Los Indios dancers (from left) Jacob Reta, Nathan Paz, Jasper Zapata, Shilo Payne, and Antonio Narvaez participate in the January 1, 2014, celebration as Monarca Martín Barela looks on at La Capilla, where La Virgen will stay for the year.

One the facing page, Ernie Misquez is pictured in front, with Frank Marta dancing behind him.

Corporation dancers and members conclude the first day of the year with more dances and a short gathering to acknowledge participants and their contributions in the Casa del Pueblo, the meeting house and spiritual home of the community. Whoops of joy, hugs, and laughter erupt during the La Rueda (left) the round dance, that welcomes all to join.

Mayordomos lead the monthly Rosary before La Virgen in La Capilla or the grotto dedicated to the antepasados (ancestors)

"The rosaries got started in 1951 because my dad, Miguel, was real sick with double pneumonia. And my dad had a sister, my aunt Tia Maria, who decided to have a rosary every Sunday night at the Capilla for my dad while he was in the hospital. So we would go and pray the rosary, but my dad passed away in September. They would continue praying it the Sunday closest to the 12th. And there was this lady Chepa — Josefa Salcedo, who was Henry's aunt and Ernesto's (Dominguez) sister, who led the rosaries."   — Pablo Fierro

"Sometime later the rosary date was changed to the 12th of the month. Pablo also said that he has only missed the rosary once, for our cousin's wedding."   — Dominic Fierro

The faithful join in praying the Rosary inside the small oratorio (La Capilla) in this 1991 photo.

"We cannot forget our antepasados. Without our ancestors we would not be here or have these traditions. To me, it's all about family."
— Miguel Parra

During the warmer months or when La Capilla is not open, the outdoor Altár de Nuestros Antepasados provides a place for prayer and reflection. Rev. Vincent Peterson, O.F.M. Conv., (photo at right) gives a blessing during the dedication ceremony after the grotto was completed in September 2009.

El Cerco: January's traditional Tiwa rabbit hunt

Photo by Jose Luis Nevarez

Capitánes Joe Raymond Fierro, Ed Fierro, and Michael Molinar await the 2013 ceremony before the rabbit hunt as the Humero, Reymundo Molinar, blesses their varas, or ceremonial staffs, in the smoke of the sacred fire.

Damario Pedraza, a Capitán during the 2009 Cerco, paints the face of Delia Salayandia before the hunt begins.

At dawn on a brisk winter morning, smoke curls skyward from a patch of native vegetation bounded by pecan orchards and Interstate 10. It signals the location of the rabbit hunt, a gathering of Pueblo residents and Corporation members who follow the rituals of El Cerco.

Families gather, stake out their portion of the desert near the flameless fire and walk with gifts of creosote branches. Women also present fat "cigarillos" of tobacco wrapped in corn husk to the Humero, the man who tends this sacred fire. He takes the hand-made cigarettes from the women who wish to join in the hunt.

He instructs each person, from preschoolers to adults, on how to place his or her bundle of the desert shrub in the four directions atop a fragrant fog of smoke.

They retreat to one of the Capitánes to receive the three red ocher dots on cheeks and chin (women) or lines on either side of the nose (men) of the paint that signify they are ready for the hunt.

Before participants head out, they receive their instructions from the Humero, and rabbits are thanked for the food they will provide.

The Humero performs a ceremony and presents a vara. (ceremonial staff of native tree branches) to each of the war captains overseeing the hunt.

The hunters form a large circle, beating the yucca and bushes with their sticks of mesquite wood (garrotes) and chanting to startle the rabbits, caught by hand or brought down with the expertly thrown traditional weapon.

Death is swift with a quick blow to the neck, and females — unless a woman is the person catching the rabbit — rush to claim the prey, which the first will "buy" with homemade empanadas during lunch.

The morning passes quickly as the rabbit is spotted, chased in a frenzied dash over prickly terrain, and is either captured or disappears down a hole or sprints into the distance. Some years yield 20 or more animals; others there are only one or two.

The ongoing drought in the winter of 2014 produced "Rabbits: two (those that escaped) and Indians: zero," laughs Capitán Miguel Parra on his way back to camp for lunch. Meals of fried rabbit or chile con conejo are unlikely.

El Cerco, which also means fence or barrier, is a time for families and friends to visit, appreciate the surroundings of their ancestors, and reflect on their own childhood memories. Several members were raised in this Ft. Fillmore area, a frontier outpost important in the Civil War. Elders say a drought in the 1800s forced their ancestors to move from Ysleta near El Paso to this spot in order to farm — and survive.

"I was born in Ft. Fillmore, N.M., in the home of Pablo Fierro; my mom and his mother were sisters. My mother used to cook for the 12th of December — she was in charge of the macaroni and cheese," says Jose Luis Nevarez. "When I joined the Corporation, I started taking pictures of the activities, which I enjoy. I even got on top of the church steeple to get some shots!"

A monument of volcanic rocks and a separated, small cemetery exist there now, but the people still notice the hawks that circle overhead. They point out the medicinal herbs, along with the ailments they cure, that remain on the traditional hunting ground.

Photo by Jose Luis Nevarez

Johnny Hernandez presents a smoke-blessed vara to his brother, Ray, before the hunt.

Nicolas M. Zepeda (right) rolls tobacco in corn husks to prepare cigarillos for the Humero.

Pueblo member Antonio Fierro (facing page) teaches Lydia Jones how to place creosote branches atop the fire. Behind them others wait their turn: Arianna, Bella, Gabby, and Andrea Fierro are joined by Joe Loera, and Capitánes Joe Raymond Fierro and Michael Moliner. Humero is Reymundo Molinar during the 2010 rabbit hunt.

"The rabbit hunt is a special event; the cantos have be right and have to be in order. The rabbit symbolizes how good your year would be. The people make the cerco. If the people form a circle, there is happiness and food for life, and without the circle there is no food — there's failure."   — Henry Narvaez

"It's not so much catching the rabbits, for me, anymore. It's more about traditions, which are important to show our grandkids and community."   — Robert Parra

Bianca Paz and her niece, Angeni Paz, use garrotes to flush rabbits from the brush (above).

Carolina Carabajal sits at the site of Fort Fillmore, remembering her childhood, where she and her siblings played within the Civil War outpost's crumbling adobe walls, often finding buttons and artifacts from soldiers and her ancestors. The plaque on the boulders that designate the location reads, "Site of Fort Fillmore 1851-1862; In Memory of Lt. John Salopek 1921-2002."

"Rabbit hunt – we are one of the last pueblos to do this – it's an important tradition to continue. The symbolism is of working together to get fed."
— Patrick Narvaez

Young men run through the brush and jump over shrubs after a rabbit is spotted.

Miquel Parra ties a rabbit for carrying (left).

At right, Rafael "Buddy" Paz shows his newly captured rabbit to his son, Felipe.

"Howe!" Sonia Lazos celebrates the rabbit she captured during the 2013 Cerco.

Capitánes join the Humero and Cacique in prayer before the noon meal that participants have provided. From top center and clockwise are Henry Narvaez, Patrick Narvaez, Frank Narvaez, Miguel Parra, Junshiro Molinar, Ed Fierro, Joe Raymond Fierro, Reymundo Molinar, and Michael Molinar. The "Humero's Table" invites those who have nothing to eat to join the officials.

Miquel Parra and Felipe Chavez visit with Charlotte Priestly Martin, known as "Carlotta," who owns the traditional hunting grounds near Tortugas. "They are welcome here. I think it's important that the Tortugas people continue to observe their traditions," she says.

Clay drums accompany winter's social dance, El Baile de Olla

All ages celebrate during this winter dance, when kids and those who know the traditional rhythms and involved sequence of steps dance for the fun of it, taking a break to smash cascarones (confetti-filled eggshells) over heads or in a good-natured slap on the back.

"This is known as a house dance, a haunchi, which is another name we call it here," explains Michael Molinar. "It serves the same function as the Cerco — a chance to get together. I learned the song from my two grandpas, Patricio Gonzales and Pedro Pedraza, But there were many, one of them in Spanish and made up on the spot

that mocked people at the dance."

"Oh, they used to be wild and last way past midnight," remembers Margie Lazos. "It wasn't for kids, like it is now, because there was drinking — even fights would break out. Everyone had a good time, but it's good that it's a family event now."

"The filas (lines) used to be huge. As long as I can, I'll do it. It's good my son drums now; I hope this continues," Molinar adds.

"We may not have the dance if there has been a death in the Pueblo," adds David Fierro. "Then, we would ask for the family's permission."

During the 2006 Baile de Olla, families gather in the Casa del Pueblo to dance well into the night. In the image to the left, dancers Margie Lazos, Cacique Henry Narvaez, Patrick Narvaez, P.J. Narvaez, and Andrea Arellanes follow Dolores Levesque, her son, Francisco Rayos, and Sonia Lazos in lines of four.

Above, a line of male dancers (Phillip Paz, Francisco Rayos, and Michael Molinar face female partners, with Fermina Paz teaching the dancers.

Top: Iashire Molinar reacts when her father, Michael, smashes a cascarone on his own head.

Father and son Junshiro (above left; top second from left) and Michael Molinar (in plaid shirt) still drum and sing during January 2015's Baile de Olla, nine years later. Also pictured above is singer David Ferrales, Jr., while PJ Narvaez is on the left and Phillip Paz beats the drum on the right (top).

Steven Castillo breaks a confetti-filled egg on his grandmother, Sally Gonzales, in the Casa del Pueblo during the most recent Baile de Olla (top left), while Manuel Apodaca (top right) laughs as he witnesses the fun.

Dancers Marta and Francisco Lozano (left) join Miguel and Melody Parra in the dance (below). "One thing for sure is that we always have a good time," Miguel Parra says. Reymundo Molinar, who has served as Capitán de la Guerra, Humero, and a Mayordomo during his lifetime at Tortugas, reminds dancers, "Watch, learn, and do this right; it's important — the children will remember."

It takes a village – to feed one. Pueblo Mayordomos host enchilada dinners as Fiesta fundraisers in La Casa de Comida.

Dominic Fierro, above, hands two made-to-order enchilada plates to Clarissa Portillo to serve the crowd in 2013.

Katie Chavez (left) chops piles of onions during a Jubilee event that celebrated 75 years of incorporation in 1989.

Lupe Dominguez Flores and 2014 Mayordomo Bill Acosta (far left) fry eggs to top the hundreds of enchilada plates prepared at least twice a year.

Jeannette Castillo, Sylvia Padilla, Christine Misquez, Bertha Telles, Dolores Molinar, Irene Gonzales, and Sally Gonzales (from left) work in the kitchen as the Corporation observes its 100-year anniversary in the top photo (facing page).

"I have always enjoyed working the enchilada events – and also on the evening of December 10th, working in the kitchen to prepare food for the Danzantes and the people attending the Fiesta."
— Connie Ferrales

"I started coming to the Fiesta ever since I can remember. I worked in the kitchen for numerous events, and I always enjoy doing anything I can. This is very spiritual for me. This is what I was taught by my parents. This is my life, and I'm proud to be a part of this Corporation."
— Rosemary Herrera Aguilar

Native plants create unique mementos, ramos, for Palm Sunday

Pablo Fierro holds a finished cross he made in 2009 that forms the frame for "palms" to be handed out to the people attending services on Palm Sunday. Corporation members gather the plants and spend the week before Easter crafting these ramos made from tree branches, sotol cups, and sabino – fragrant evergreen boughs.

Deacon Al Bowers carries the monstrance (castoria), which holds the host during Holy Communion, that is made from pearly sotol cups and native vegetation for the Palm Sunday Mass. From right, Abraham Ceballos, Rev. Giles Carie, O.F.M. Conv., and Juanita Del Rio walk to the Sanctuario de Nuestra Señora de Guadalupe in a short procession from the parish hall in 2009.

Miguel Parra (facing page) crafts ramos.

Tessie Apodaca (above left) specializes in making small versions of the ramos so that all may have one. "When I arrived a little late one time, I was given only one of the sotal cups," she explains in 2014, when Pauline Pachecho also creates her own distinctive ramos to be shared with family members (center).

Henry Narvaez and Fred Salas carefully place candelarias on the altar before Mass in 1990 (right).

"Desde el cielo una hermosa mañana..."
(From heaven one beautiful morning...)

So begins the hymn that tells of Our Lady's apparitions in Mexico in 1531:

Early one December morning, Juan Diego, a humble indigenous man, heard beautiful singing, a divine harmony, as he walked near Tepeyac, a mountain in his path into town. Looking upward, he saw an incredible sight — a beautiful woman descending from the heavens, bathed in light.

"Su llegada lleno de Alergria, de Luz y Harmonia, todo el Anahuac"

As he approached, he noticed that she was dressed "like the sun" illuminating the entire Anahuac valley. She wore garments decorated in a manner familiar to his people; even her robe was of a color favored by the locals.

And, she spoke to him in the native Nahuatl language: "Juanito, Juan Diegito."

She identified herself as the ever-Virgen Mary, Mother of the True God. She had selected that site for a church to be built in Her honor and asked that Juan Diego take that message to the Bishop (Don Fray Juan de Zumarraga). Unfortunately, the Bishop did not believe Juan Diego's story and told him to return the next day.

On that Sunday, Juan Diego returned to the Bishop, who sent him away, commanding him not to return until he had proof that the message was "real."

Juan Diego delivered the message to Our Lady, who told Juan Diego to return the next day. However, finding his uncle ill and very close to death, Juan Diego did not return: he spent the entire day with his uncle.

The following day, Tuesday, December 12th, Juan Diego started out on his journey to find a priest for his uncle's last rites. Leaving very early while it was still dark, he decided to go "around" the mountain, knowing that if he met up with Our Lady, he would be obligated

to do as She asked. However, Our Lady intercepted him and asked him where he was going.

Juan Diego related the story of his gravely ill uncle and asked that Our Lady be patient: he would return to Her for whatever signal She wished to send to the Bishop.

"Listen, Juan Diego and take this into your heart. Am I not here, who is your mother?"

Our Lady spoke to Juan Diego, reassuring him of the love and care She had for him, for all her children. She reassured Juan Diego that his uncle would be well.

She then sent him to gather some flowers. Juan Diego did as She asked, knowing full well that December is not the season for flowers in that area.

He found a "paradise" with flowers of all kinds and colors; indeed, their aroma was everywhere. He returned to Our Lady, who took the flowers in Her hands: She directed Juan Diego to take them, as the sign, to the Bishop, who would recognize Her wish for a temple. She also told Juan Diego that she would "glorify" his role in being her messenger.

"En la tilma con rosas pintadas, Su imagen amada se digno dejar."

Juan Diego returned to the Bishop, carrying the multitude of flowers in his tilma; as the flowers spilled unto the floor, the Bishop and other clergy around him knelt in the realization of the validity of the message. Our Lady's image appeared on Juan Diego's tilma, "stamped" in the same form and fashion as it still appears on that tilma in the Cathedral of Mexico City.

Desde el cielo una hermosa manana...

I was introduced to this hymn long before I started school; perhaps, during infancy when I went to the Fiesta to watch my father dance every year. It was this hymn that my mother suggested I remember whenever I felt the need for comfort, especially at times when she was ill. "Remember la cancion de Mama Lupe."

"No estoy aqui yo que soy tu Madre?...no soy yo la fuente de tu alegeria?"

Mama Lupe. What else could She be but la Mama Grande, La Verdadera Madre of us all? I am not sure when I fully realized what Mama Lupe's words truly meant: I do remember that before age 12, I was already aware of all that Mama Lupe was doing to take care of Her children. I got insight into Her Love whenever I spent time in Tortugas, and whenever I sat with the other malinches and we listened to the adults talk about the milagros Mama Lupe had done for the danzantes, bailadoras, and the many people who came for the pilgrimage to Tortugas Mountain.

I lost my mother while I was still in my teens but I often remembered her words, her lessons about Mama Lupe. I carried Mama Lupe, and Tortugas, always with me through college (I still danced as a bailadora), when I went off to "see the world" far from home, and through my daughters' early lives. They were 4 and 2 years old when I was finally able to introduce them to the Fiesta, but they already knew about Mama Lupe.

Now, my grandchildren are learning. "Mama Lupe's" song is their lullaby of choice, and several months ago, I caught the familiar melody as my granddaughter hummed it while she played with her toys. As always, when my own mama comes to me in dreams, she is always the one who is leading me to see Mama Lupe, whether it is as a reflection in a river, crossing a bridge to resolve a problem, or dancing in a Fiesta in Tortugas.

"Dame, Senora, Tu Bendicion --- (y aqui dejo mi corazon)."

— Rosemary Estrada Kirby

No one seems to know exactly how old the sacred image (facing page) is that graces the palanquin, carried through the village during the Fiesta, but Corporation members say they remember it from their childhoods and that it has been reframed more than once in order to preserve it. "It's still vibrant because it is not exposed to direct light," says Dominic Fierro. Her image is also reproduced in Tortugas buildings, homes and outdoor altars, as well as on the tilma, or cloak, of the sculpture by renowned artist Sonny Rivera depicting Juan Diego (above), located on the church grounds. St. Juan Diego Cuauhtlatoatzin, was named the first Roman Catholic indigenous saint in 2002.

San Juan Fiesta honors first patron saint of Tortugas

Kelly Kirby (right) dances in a circle before the Vigin of Guadalupe's palanquin, which remains in the Capilla during the San Juan Fiesta. Joining her (counter clockwise) are Antonio Parra, Ralph Paz, Francis Wood, Becky Rios-Chavez, and Jeannette Castillo.

Southern New Mexico's summer heat challenges Los Indios dancers each June 24 as they remember San Juan Bautista, for whom the original village of San Juan de Dios was named. They dance in front of the Sanctuario de Nuestra Señora de Guadalupe before attending a church service and visiting the Virgin's image in La Capilla and honoring her with dance outside. "We made a commitment when San Juan and Guadalupe came together to honor Saint John on June 24," explains 2014 Capitán de Guerra Ed Fierro.

In the predawn darkness on St. John's Day, some Pueblo residents welcome the day with drumming that carries throughout the village. Fermina Paz beats her handmade drum, and it's answered by one of her sisters, Carolina Carabajal or Margie Lazos. "When I want to pray outside, I drum," Fermina says.

Arturo Moya and Jackie Caballero (above) dance in front of the church in 2012.

At right, Phillip Paz, who holds the leafy vara of summertime as a Capitán, and Most Rev. Oscar Cantú, S.T.D.D.D., Bishop of the Roman Catholic Diocese of Las Cruces, watch the performance.

Los Indios dancers line up, facing the church, in reverence to the other patron saint of the Pueblo, St. John the Baptist in 2010. Unless June 24 falls on the weekend, visitors to the San Juan Turtle Fest will not see the quiet summer ceremony.

Jacob Reta and partner Irene Gonzales perform the traditional sequence of steps in the photo at right.

"Do you know how Tortugas got its name?"

After posing this question, Frank Gonzales, whose Tortugas roots stretch back to his grandfather, Saturnino Gonzales, is quick to answer: "There used to be a lake just west of the village, and it was full of turtles."

He says his "whole clan" settled in the community, and he fondly remembers hearing the stories about how wagons and buggies with wooden wheels would drive through the water to swell the wood.

Sometimes this was an instant fix for the rattles and ill-fitting rims that come with southern New Mexico's dry climate. Shovels, hoes, and other farm implements would also get a soaking in order to better fit their metal heads.

Juan B. Montoya, 101 years old in 2014, actually saw that lake when he was a youngster growing up in the community of San Juan. The river (Rio Grande) flowed near the lake that was located in a depression alongside what is now South Main Street where a convenience store stands.

His parents, Josefa Vasquez and Juan Montoya, settled in the village before New Mexico's statehood in 1912.

"There were so many turtles around, you would trip over them when you walked at night," Montoya confirms. "And some of them were big!" In his younger days, he says, he spent a lot of time removing cottonwoods from the nearby river bosque that was converted to farmland.

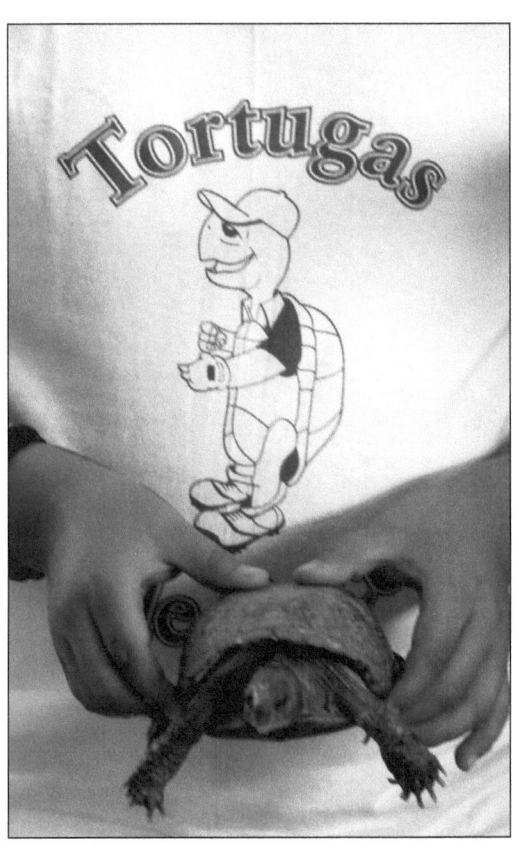

On the Sundat close to June 24, eager turtle jockeys race their reptiles each year in the Tortugas Pueblo's popular Turtle Fest competition for the grand prize of $50.

San Juan FiestaTurtlefest raises funds for parish

In 1988, brothers-in-law David Fierro and Frank Torres decided to initiate turtle races, along with other activities, to help support the Shrine and Parish of Our Lady of Guadalupe. They built a simple track and found eight turtles for the first competition that draws 140-160 pet turtles today. The event was an instant success, and proceeds help pay expenses for the church that serves communities around Las Crucces.

Competition is fierce during the Tortugas Turtle Races, held the weekend closest to San Juan Bautista's Day, June 24. In addition to the races, there is a golf tournament and tardeada Saturday and Sunday.

At left, celebrity judges Rev. Vincent Peterson, O.F.M. Conv., Nathan Small, Emily Guerra, Mary Helen Garcia, and J. Paul Taylor name the winner of the 2013 contest.

In the top photo, Jacob Padilla, 3, gets ready to race his turtle in the 2006 event.

Continuing in the tradition: Tortugas pottery, drums

Among the vintage photographs in the Casa de Comida, there is one titled "Tortugas Potter" that features the image of Luz Duran, who brought her knowledge of ceramics to Tortugas when she settled in the community 100 years ago.

Fermina Paz (left) and Carolina Carabajal treasure some of these original, utilitarian pieces that were sold in Mesilla after being packed in straw for the bumpy wagon ride to the nearby community.

The sisters learned from their "Mama Luz" and are passing the coil techniques on to their children and grandchildren. They also display some of their own

pots in the image below.

The potters still remember the location of good sources of clay in the nearby desert, where they sift a handful to examine the texture and taste it, as they were instructed as children. Fermina and Carolina have also created exquisite Nativity figures.

"Every time Mama Luz would make a pot, she would burn some plants and say a prayer. Every time she would go get clay, she said you have to leave something — some corn meal, beans, whatever you have," Fermina recalls. "And we thank Mother Earth and Father Sky for whatever we have."

The Cacique holds the old Tombé when it not being played during the Fiesta.

Tortugas elders and 1982 Fiesta officials encircle the drum as they sing the chants for Los Indios dancers in the image below. From left, Pedro Gonzales, Ignacio Peña, Pedro Pedraza, and Sammy Romero taught the rituals to many of the current Pueblo members.

Used only for ceremonial purposes, the sacred drum, El Tombé, is described as the heartbeat of the Pueblo, and there are rules for its use and handling. The Capitán de la Guerra bears responsibility for the old drum, brought from Ysleta del Sur when members moved north and settled in Tortugas.

"The Tombé is very precious to us," says David Ferrales, Jr., who has taken on that responsibility as Capitán. "If anything ever happened to it, it would be devastating."

"We all grew up making drums," says Sonia Lazos, pointing to those hanging in her mother's home.

Younger Pueblo members watched and learned how to select the proper tree trunk, carve out the interior, then prepare and stretch cow or deer hide over the hollow log and secure it with rawhide strings.

"You need a lot of strength to do it," adds Irene Payne, who tells a story about her hands repeatedly cramping while stretching the hide.

COMMUNITY EVENTS
Tortugas, NMSU host tribal gatherings

New Mexico State University's Indian Studies Program connects Tortugas Pueblo with other tribes in the state. The village has hosted two recent seminars with members of the Los Comanches de la Serna from Ranchos de Taos, pictured above. The northern New Mexico group also shared dance traditions with Los Indios in front of the Sanctuario de Nuestra Señora de Guadalupe in 2009.

Like Los Indigenes de Nuestra Señora de Guadalupe, Los Comanches de la Serna also honor the Virgin.

Young Jonathan Wood watches the elaborate leaps and moves members of the Ranchos de Taos group execute at left.

Below, Los Indios dancers learn a new dance from Los Comanches in 2009.

Cacique and Pueblo members celebrate San Ysidro Day

Before the ceremony in 2013 (top image, facing page), Arturo Montoya and Henry Narvaez invite Farm and Ranch Museum Director Mark Santiago (third from left) to beat one of the Pueblo's handcrafted drums. Patrick Narvaez holds the drum at right.

Narvaez and other Pueblo members participate each year, with Antonio Avalos, Kathy Paz and Felipe Paz (from right) in the top image above.

Girls dressed in white toss rose petals in the acequia (irrigation ditch) that brings life-giving water to crops at the Farm and Ranch Heritage Museum in Las Cruces.

"We believe the smoke carries our prayers to the creator," says Henry Narvaez, the spiritual leader of Tortugas Pueblo.

He lifts a cigarillo, made in the traditional manner — tobacco rolled in a corn husk. The Cacique then requests onlookers face the four directions with him as he asks for blessings during the opening ceremony at the New Mexico Farm and Ranch Heritage Museum's San Ysidro observance, which honors the patron saint of farmers each spring.

Pueblo participation during "The Blessing of the Fields" began in 2001, when Los Indios President/ board member Felipe Chavez worked at the museum near Tortugas Mountain.

Tortugas history recognized during Las Cruces Centennial

"The parade gave us an opportunity to reenact our original procession.

"Our ancestors would start at St. Genevieve's and go south on Main to Lohman, turn left and go down Church Street and then back to St. Gen.

"The parade that we joined followed part of the original procession route."

— Henry Narvaez

Members constructed a float for the 2012 parade through downtown Las Cruces. Joe Herrerra, Santana Ferrales, Peter Ferrales, Marcela Ferrales, and Iashire Molinar wave to the crowd; Patrick and Henry Narvaez join Reymundo Molinar on drum.

Tortugas Pueblo members and village residents attend dedication of new courtroom that bears its name in 2013

Photos (2) by Jose Luis Nevarez

"It is important because the court house is very near to where the Indios became established about one block away (and almost exactly 100 years ago). It was almost like closing the circle. The Indios have come full circle, back home."

— Henry Narvaez

Witness to history: Those attending the dedication of the Tortugas Courtroom climb the stairs of the new facility.

Outside of the new courtroom, Pueblo members play the drum and chant, while others dance. Pictured around the Tombé are Antonio Avalos, Arturo Montoya, Henry and Patrick Narvaez, and Felipe Chavez.

Los Danzantes invited to National Hispanic Cultural Center

In the photo above, Los Danzantes members dance "El Paño," being led by Milo Reyes, serving as Monarca, and Malinche Alicia Bronson, while Monarcas Peter Ferrales and Ernesto Misquez watch from the back.

Top right, Malinche Marcie Ferrales accompanies the group as Peter Ferrales dances as Monarca.

The small group that was able to travel from Tortugas to join their Cacique Henry Narvaez (center) in Albuquerque.

Identified Danzantes (third from left to right), Joe Herrerra, Miguel Silva, and Dario Silva are pictured with Monarcas Ernesto Misquez and Peter Ferrales, Narvaez, Alicia Bronson, Monarca Paul Herrera, Marcie Ferrales, violinist Leo Perez, Santana Ferrales, and Milo Reyes, Monarca Assistant.

In 2008, Los Danzantes were among nine groups in New Mexico invited to participate in "Matachines!" at Albuquerque's National Hispanic Cultural Center. The two-day gathering featured historical presentations and performances by groups representing Cochiti, Raramuri, Yaqui, Alcalde, Picuris, Bernalillo, Tijeras, and Jemez Pueblo.

The program was funded by the National Endowment for the Arts and its American Masterpieces Program. Tortugas dancers were well received, and it was an opportunity for four members who serve as Monarcas to oversee the small group of six Danzantes able to attend. Two of those, Ernesto Misquez and Peter Ferrales, have since died.

The nine Matachine groups displayed varied style of dance and dress and danced in the plaza area of the Center.

"Will you be my relevo?"

"Yes, of course. Thank you for asking."

There is a whole ceremony to asking someone to be a relevo for the following year: it involves a formal visit, perhaps a gift, and a short run-down of the year-long responsibilities.

Usually, it also takes some coaxing and waiting, sometimes a long time, for the person to think about what he or she is getting into.

And, there are also the requirements: the most serious is that the Mayordomos should be a married couple. As a "single," I had not even entertained the idea or hope that someday I would be accepted as a Mayordoma. It happened twice.

"You will? That was easy."

"La Virgencita has never said "no" whenever or whatever I ask Her, even if She answers my prayers in ways I don't expect. Why should I say "no" to Her? I will serve Her in any way I can."

Being one of the Mayordomas can be a lonely role but there is always that overwhelming realization: all of it is being done to serve — Our Lady, the Pueblo, the general public and, very important, the ancestors. But, when help is really needed, it is the Pueblo and the general public that appear to help — to serve.

There are so many interesting aspects to being Mayordoma but one of the best has to be the opportunity to decide, along with the other mayordomos, how to "dress" the Virgencita (and Her palanquin), as well as the Casa de Comida and Casa del Pueblo.

Rosemary Estrada Kirby, Mayordoma in 2009, cradles her granddaughter, Isis Kirby Spitzig, in the Casa de Comida.

And, this brings to the forefront something extremely important: all about the Fiesta (and about the Pueblo) reflects the union of two different cultural traditions; the intermingling of Spanish and Native American cultures: the richness of European religion and indigenous spirituality.

Fortunately, all of my "compañeros" agreed to go with our native ancestors' motif -- using décor from nature and colors reflecting such.

I think it should be a definite requirement that every member should serve on the Board of Directors, dance in one of groups, climb the cerro, and be a Mayordomo/Mayordoma — all at least once. Although each is a unique experience and lends us a different perspective, it is in being a Mayordomo that we get insight into the enormity — the BIGNESS — of what this is all about. Each allows us moving moments.

I agree with my compañera, Arianna Fierro: Watching the expressions on people's faces, their unabashed tears, the physical pain that some endure to kneel or bend — I don't think anyone could remain unmoved.

I wouldn't trade all that experience for anything ... which is why my reply, five years later, was exactly the same:

"Will you be my relevo?"

"Yes, of course."

— Rosemary Estrada Kirby

Being Mayordomos: A great honor and privilege

Connie Ferrales (center) helps 1991 Mayordomos Felipe and Katie Chavez, and Frank Torres, whose wife, Patsy, works with volunteers in the background, decorate "their" Virgin in La Capilla.

"During the October and November months Tortugas becomes your second home," says Arianna Fierro. "There is always something going on and things that need to get done, such as making red chile, help make biscochos, work parties that involve cleaning the Casa de Comida and the Pueblo grounds."

Throughout the year they also take turns cleaning the church and leading the monthy rosary. Mayordoma Rosie Stewart points out, "It entails a lot of work, but it is very rewarding — something everyone should experience at least once."

"I enjoy it! It's a wonderful experience," says Katie Chavez, "knowing you have accomplished all this - decorating La Capilla and the Casa del Pueblo, making sure everything goes on schedule, providing programs, cooking food. If you survive it, that is."

Tortugas Pueblo prepares for Día Doce

Weeks before La Fiesta de Nuestra Señora de Guadalupe begins, Tortugas bustles with activity as Pueblo members clean the grounds and the church, La Capilla, Casa del Pueblo, and Casa de Comida. After receiving a permit and an approved location from the Bureau of Land Management, sotol plants are gathered (left) for the construction of quiotes, or walking sticks, during the pilgrimage on Tortugas Mountain each December 11.

At the bottom of the facing page, Frank Ferrales and another Pueblo member clear vegetation near Pueblo buildings.

At right, Mayordoma Patsy Torres and her young daughter, Lorena, clean the image of the Virgin and La Capilla.

Frank Ferrales sweeps red chile that dries in the sun on the roof of La Casa de Comida (1991). The chile is used for red enchilada sauce and also the Chile Colorado served during the Feast on December 12.

Fiesta begins with
El Velorio, night-long confirmation of faith

Los Danzantes await their turn to visit the Virgin before the procession (above).

Mayordomos Daniel Flores and Frank Torres remove the image for the procession as a large crowd gathers outside the little chapel where the image is kept throughout the year (lower right).

As darkness descends on December 10, activity increases in the normally quiet village of Tortugas. For several frenzied weeks Mayordormos, the Fiesta sponsors for the year, have coordinated efforts to ensure everything falls into place so that Pueblo members and all who wish to honor the "Mother of the Americas" can observe the three sacred days devoted to Her.

Although the evening is a time when friends and family, many of whom have not seen each other for a year or longer, can reunite, it is also a solemn occasion.

A Monarca receives a Native American blessing with smoke at the home altar of a Pueblo relative before joining his fellow Danzantes at La Escuelita for the hushed walk to La Capilla. Mayordomos, the parish priest, and a choir await with the image of the Virgin. She is newly "dressed" for the year and ready for Her celebration. Muted strains of music, hymns sung in Spanish accompanied by guitar, can be heard behind the closed door.

At the appointed time, it is opened and illumination streams from the doorway — a sacred spotlight on the Danzantes, Malinches, and people eagerly waiting in the cold. Each Danzante kneels in front of the palanquin, praying to Her for a successful Fiesta and a personal request all his own.

Choir members (from left) Martín Serecerez, Mike and Bernice Navarro, singers, Richard Silva, Burt Silva, and Joe DiMatteo at right serenade the image of Nuestra Señora de Guadalupe in La Capilla before She is carried to La Casa del Pueblo for El Velorio on December 10, 2013.

Photo by Jose Luis Nevarez

"As a Mayordomo, the most moving part for me was being in the Capilla and watching everyone come and sort of profess and pray to the Virgin," says Arianna Fierro, vice president of La Corporación.

"You can almost physically see people unburden themselves in front of Her and ask for help, health and give thanks. It is a very moving experience," she reflects.

The 12-18 dancers and Malinches then return to the night and assume position in two lines to escort the image and Fiesta officials to the nearby Casa del Pueblo in a candle-lit procession.

In choreography that dates back generations, the Danzantes approach the image dos y dos (two by two), bow, turn in opposite directions and retreat to the end of the line.

"My fondest memory is seeing the Virgin for the first time on December 10th. It appears She is smiling! I also appreciate any time the Corporation remembers our ancestors. For we are nothing without their sacrifices and efforts."
— David Fierro

Blasts from a shotgun loaded with blank cartridges shatter the cold winter air after all have completed the cycle and begin their approach again. The armed men are known as the custodias, and they signal a change of dances and the ceremony throughout the night, but the noise is said to dispel evil spirits — "and it's also in jubilation," says David Fierro.

Mayordomos from the present year are joined by those who will take their places in the coming year, with the men supporting the four corners of the image that is carefully placed at the west end of La Casa del Pueblo, slightly below the permanent image of the patroness, who seems to be looking at those gathered in the meeting hall.

Once the novena, dedicated to the Virgin of Guadalupe, is completed, the Danzantes fill the center of the building to dance. Their measured steps propel them forward and backward and end with a stamp of the foot, dancing in time to the violinist, Leo Perez. Los Danzantes will perform two of their dances – "La Entrada" and "La Batalla," only this one evening, explains member Eric Fierro.

Monarca Martín Barela describes the night and the entire Fiesta as a "big experience." From the time he joined Los Danzantes in 1987, he says, "It felt close to my heart, always very faithful to the traditions." His is a lifetime position of leading Los Danzantes. "I'm in this for the long haul, as long as my health continues. I was chosen for a reason."

Outside, the Humero lights the first of the ceremonial fires that he tends throughout the Fiesta.

Participants dwindle as the hours pass, but individuals kneel at the feet of the Virgin's image to pray throughout the evening and well into the early morning hours; breaks occur when Danzantes dance at appointed times, as well as for refreshments and cocoa served in the Casa de Comida about 10:30 p.m.

The cena, a hearty stew accompanied by green chile, beans and pan indio (Indian bread), is provided at midnight for the dancers and those attending El Velorio, the night watch. Cooks also prepare burritos for Pueblo Capitànes and the Humero to take on the pilgrimage up "A" Mountain that begins in the early morning on December 11.

Mayordomos Rafael "Buddy" Paz and Raymond Tellez (top photo) take the image into the building, where She will be honored during El Velorio.

People gather in the Casa del Pueblo to pray to the Virgin.

Los Danzantes honor the Virgin of Guadalupe with dance

"I remember being at the Fiesta with my great grandmother Rafaela Dominguez when I was about 3 years old. I was fascinated with the Danzantes and loved the music.

"Then, when I was a little older, when I got tired on December 10th, my dad (Ernesto Dominguez) would wrap me in blankets and leave me in the car to sleep — that was just a fact of life of being at the Fiesta. But I never felt neglected; I was always surrounded by family and friends.

"I danced as a Malinche at 6 until I was 11 — I was taller than the Monarca, Fred Salas! He was a friend of my dad's, and I would just stick to him."

— Guadalupe Dominguez Flores

Los Danzantes enter the Casa del Pueblo and dance at regular intervals throughout the evening. Danzante members include Joe Raymond Fierro (left), Malinche Katherine Parra, and Monarca Ernesto Misquez (left).

The male dancers kneel on the concrete floor and pray shortly after entering the building on December 10 (above).

Los Danzantes and the public continue to honor the Virgin of Guadalupe until La Alba, the Dawn Ceremony held early December 11.

The faithful kneel in front of the Virgin's image, light candles, and pray in the Casa del Pueblo, open all night and early morning on December 10 and 11 in 2004. The crowd is welcomed to the Casa de Comida late in the evening and again at midnight for snacks and a meal.

In the top right image Sylvia, Robert, and their son, Robert, Jr., present Malinche Katherine Parra with a birthday cake in 2006 during the first break. In 2014, she worked at the community dining hall helping to serve the noon meal on December 12. The kitchens in the Casa de Comida are busy throughout the three-day Fiesta.

At right, Katie Chavez, Philly Dickson, and Sylvia Parra joke with each other while making tortillas for the Capitánes and Fiesta officials to eat during the pilgrimage.

"I always thought making tortillas was a chore. Now that we make burritos for the Capitánes on December 10th, I feel this is an honor, not a chore."
— Bertha Tellez

Danzantes continue to dance throughout the night and early morning.

Before dawn, the faithful join in a procession that begins La Alba (dawn) ceremony when Mayordomos welcome the new day and deliver the image to the Sanctuario de Nuestra Señora de Guadalupe, where She can be visited until the late afternoon of January 1 of the following year.

Without a wink of sleep, many of these people who attended the entire Velorio prepare for the pilgrimage that begins in an hour.

Mayordomos Christine Misquez and Lawrence Jimenez (left) lead the candlelight procession from the Casa del Pueblo to the Sanctuario with fellow 2013 Mayordomos Dominic Fierro and Kelly Kirby, well before dawn on December 11.

December 11: "I Feel Closer to God..."

So reads a message from a young Pueblo member, Cipriano Castillo, Jr., who prefaces these words with: "I've hiked this mountain at least 1,000 times in my life, but only on the 11th of December do I carry my own and my family's promises to the top. I am overwhelmed with humility and love."

Still sleepy from spending the prior evening in prayer or rising before dawn on this frigid morning, those wishing to join the Pueblo's pilgrimage to the top of Tortugas Mountain (also referred to as "A" Mountain for NMSU's Aggies) huddle in the relative warmth of the Casa del Pueblo. That's when the stories begin...

"They didn't used to allow women to climb the mountain in pants — they had to wear dresses," says the middle-aged man to my left. "My grandpa climbed until he was 80, something he did as his 'promesa' to La Virgen de Guadalupe," another shares.

"Promesa" — the word that means a promise to fulfill a vow for blessings requested — is used in conversations throughout this day and evening.

For many, that promise involves the strenuous trip from Tortugas to the desert mountain peak, elevation 4,931 ft., and back.

"I had polio as a kid," shares David Fierro, who is proud of his father's and grandfather's participation in the Pueblo. "I was in an iron lung and everything. But with my dad's promesa and his faith, you can see that I did recover."

Before hiking to the top of Tortugas Mountain, pilgrims pray to the Virgin of Guadalupe, often making a vow or promesa. They visit the image tha has been placed in the church after El Velorio.

After hikers have registered for the trek, they assemble around the Capitánes and Cacique for El Camino, the ceremony of the path. Using coals from the ceremonial bonfire lit the night before, Henry Narvaez lights a cigarillo that provides smoke for the blessing. The crowd faces the four directions as the Cacique offers his prayers.

Priests and the Diocese of Las Cruces Bishop join the group, which assembles dos y dos, with women always to the right of the men's lines.

A small portrait of the Virgin is carried by the Humero, whose job it is to transport Her safely to the mountain's altar and return Her to the Casa del Pueblo's Turla (kiva-like room with dirt floor used for special ceremonies).

Capitánes are charged with the safety of all who participate. The group is encouraged to stay together, be respectful, and pray the rosary on the trip to the mountain that looms larger with each step.

At its base, pilgrims chose their own path from among four routes to the top. Each has its merits, but none is easy. Some have to rest (also jokingly called "enjoying the view") more often than others. Kids scurry past older walkers and parents carrying babies and young children. A hand up is happily taken, and helping others is genuinely appreciated.

Everyone of a certain age agrees that the mountain gets taller with each passing year, as coats are shed and deep breaths of air cool burning lungs.

Those unable to walk are driven up the narrow, unstable road by volunteers who know its treacherous twists, turns and drop-offs.

Pilgrims depart Tortugas in 2014 and are led by Humero Miguel Parra, with the image of La Virgen, and Capitán Frank Narvaez. Bishop Oscar Cantú leads the faithful in the rosary in the top image.

Below, pilgrims ascend Tortugas Mountain in several inches of snow.

One of the faithful, pictured on the facing page, makes the journey without shoes as his promise to La Virgen Morena, the Dark Virgin (of Guadalupe).

Reaching the summit is always a rewarding experience. People scatter to find their own spot among the rocks and cactus to spend the day. Capitánes and the Humero retreat to their traditional camp on the south-facing slope, which is soon revealed by smoke rising from the flameless fire that sanctifies the mountain.

The Bishop conducts Mass before an altar overflowing with flowers and candles, one that incorporates stones from the Casa del Pueblo, the Casa de Comida, and the Sanctuario when it was constructed. The smaller, red altar to the north, which is also crowded with candles and offerings, is the original one.

"I used to ride up the mountain with my dad, driving priests, the Bishop, the choir, always waiting for my turn to do that. Little did I know, at age 15 and six months after getting my license, that I was up there when my dad needed help," says Felipe Nevarez. "Now I have taken over my dad's part of the drive; my son is four-and-a half, and he's hoping to help like I did."

"I enjoy driving dignitaries up "A" Mountain on December 11," agrees Ray Tellez. "It is an honor." Felipe Chavez has been coordinating Fiesta logistics for years, and the end of this day without any major injuries brings with it great relief.

Depending on the weather, the day passes quickly (sunny) or slowly (cold, windy, rain), but after Mass, much of it is consumed with the construction of quiotes, walking staffs handcrafted from the base and stalks of the sotol plant.

They can be intricate and traditional, with the pearly-smooth cups of the plant's base extending most of the way up the stalk and tied with fibers from the yucca "leaves," contain images of the Virgin and other religious items, or even shimmer with portable Christmas lights and bits of garland.

"They say the more cups you use, the more sins you have to be forgiven," jokes Margie Lazos, whose extended family is known for its distinctive quiote style. "Then God help us all!" laughs her sister Carolina Carabajal.

"I was told by my family that my grandfather used to be the one that would make the string for everyone," notes Arianna Fierro, referring to the yucca leaves that are pounded and separated into strands. "Now that he can no longer make the trip up the mountain, I gladly take on that role."

Reymundo Molinar carries the Virgin's image to the top of Tortugas Mountain in 2013, the same year this father and daughter rest alongside the path to the peak, at left.

Those who have spent the day on the mountain are invited to have their faces painted in the afternoon. "It shows that for this day, you are a member of the Pueblo. You have completed the journey," explains Michael Molinar.

The village priest usually conducts the rosary as afternoon shadows lengthen. Then, cooking fires are extinguished, belongings are stashed in backpacks, barrels of trash are hauled away, and lights begin to twinkle in Las Cruces.

Candles and flowers crowd the altar where pilgrims pray throughout the day.

Photo by Jose Luis Nevarez

Hundreds gather for the late-morning Mass in this 2013 photo. It is held each December 11 atop Tortugas Mountain. Pilgrims have been honoring the Virgin of Guadalupe on the desert peak since the mid-1800s.

At right, candles fill the small, older altar on the mountain.

Rev. Donald J. Adamski, O.F.M. Conv., hears confession before Mass is celebrated.

With the Organ Mountains as a backdrop, kids romp on Tortugas Mountain as their mother crafts quiotes made from harvested plants provided by the Pueblo and delivered to the mountain's top.

Lorena Sanchez, from Pecos, N.M., spends her afternoon on the mountain making necklaces, crafted from the sotol base's smooth cups.

Hundreds converge on the pile of quiote materials to create their own walking sticks for the trip down Tortugas Mountain (facing page).

Capitánes paint the faces of pilgrims who have completed the climb and spent the day on Tortugas Mountain in the 1990 photo above.

Some choose to descend the mountain before dusk (right). The faithful pray throughout the day at the two altars on the peak.

Above, pilgrims face a frigid wind when they begin to descend Tortugas Mountain as they walk to the Pueblo in 2006.

Humero Miguel Parra removes the image of the Virgin of Guadalupe for the trek back to Tortugas.

During the 1990s, Pueblo members keep an eye on the fire atop Tortugas Mountain and watch the lights of Las Cruces to the northwest. Years ago, tires fueled the fires, but the heavy, black smoke was an environmental concern, so only wood fires are burned now.

A hush falls over the mountain as pilgrims watch the sun slip away.

"My favorite part of the Fiesta is the procession up and down the mountain and spending time in such a sacred place. It is a cleansing of the trials and tribulations of the year and a renewal of my spirit and faith," reflects Chris Barela. He makes the pilgrimage with cousin Zeke Leyva, who celebrates his birthday each year on the mountain. Leyva says, "I have fulfilled my promesa to Nuestra Señora de Guadalupe for 50 of my 61 years."

He witnessed the change from the strict rules, which included "a sharp tongue and a swift whisk of the walking stick" to a time of too much leniency.

"They are returning now to a more civil and disciplined tone, such as leading the rosary and explaining more about why things are done," Leyva says.

After Capitánes see the bonfires burning at Tortugas, they light the fire on top of the mountain and direct the pilgrims to begin the descent — this time together on the road as the paths fade in the dim twilight.

At the base of the mountain, pilgrims gather around another bonfire, turn to the east and admire the enormous cross made from lights and fires burning on their revered peak.

Pilgrims return to Tortugas after Humero Reymundo Molinar, above, carries the image of the Virgin of Guadalupe that will be returned to the Casa del Pueblo's Turla. To his right are Patrick and Henry Narvaez with Michael Molinar. Other Pueblo members that join the front line of pilgrims are (from left) Miguel Parra, Damario Pedraza, and Junshiro Molinar.

Patrick Narvaez (below) knocks at the Casa del Pueblo door, but does not gain entry until the pilgrims retreat to the village bonfire and return two more times.

Photo by Jose Luis Nevarez

Pilgrims walk the four miles with Capitánes back to the village tired, but uplifted, from the day's outing and are greeted by a village bonfire made from yucca. The Cacique and Pueblo officials welcome them upon their return.

Three times the group is led to the doors of La Casa del Pueblo, where the Cacique or his Ayudante, Patrick Narvaez, knocks on the doors with his staff to gain entry.

His knock is unanswered until the third approach, and the doors are flung open. Quiotes are either left inside or briefly placed there, then claimed by the person who made it.

Some believe this trio of knocks on the door represent the times that Juan Diego appeared before the bishop in Mexico City when his vision of the Virgin was finally believed.

The Ensayo Real (Royal Practice) for Pueblo dancers follows, and all are invited to watch in La Casa del Pueblo. The dancers have already been rehearsing the dances for weeks prior to December 11; this is a preview of what's to come the next day.

Back at the Casa de Comida, thousands of tiny albondigas (meatballs) are being rolled in preparation for the feast. At the end of a very long day, cooks fold their aprons and promise to return early in order to feed the masses a noon meal.

Tomorrow is Día Doce, "ready or not!"

Rev. Don Adamski participates with pilgrims in the return ceremony after making the trek in 2007.

It's albondigas (meatballs) time at the Casa de Comida on the evening of December 11. Above in 2008, Philly Dickson (right) works with Ray and Sally Hernandez.

In the 1997 photo below, Stella Sanchez (left) and (right front) Sylvia Fierro, Frank Torres, Arianna Fierro, Henry Narvaez and Mary Lou Narvaez help make the thousands of small meatballs to serve during the noon feast on December 12.

Photo by Jose Luis Nevarez

My Time in La Casa de Comida, 1965-2009

I had just moved back to Las Cruces in 1965 when my uncle Margarito Fierro asked if I would help in the kitchen in La Casa de Comida. Little did I realize that period would last 44 years and that the first few years meant washing dishes, pans, wash tubs, etc.

Jose Ferrales was the main caretaker of the fire and keeping the kitchen running smoothly for the December fiesta, a job I sort of inherited when he quit working in the kitchen in the late 1960s or early 70s. The two individuals who were always around to help in the kitchen were Marciala "Chala" and her husband Pablo Fierro, who had been there long before I started (50 years ago) and are still there when needed.

The only heat in La Casa de Comida then was a fireplace and a couple of gas stoves that were on only when cooking. The fireplace was kept going during the annual fiesta for Nuestra Señora de

Pat Beckett (right) and Lupe Dominquez-Flores (center) meet a future member of Los Indigines in the kitchen of Casa de Comida before the noon meal on December 12.

Guadalupe and in the evenings of December 10-12.

A large fire of mesquite was kept burning outside of the side door and in the fireplace. These fires provided the live coals to shovel under the ollas of chile, albondigas and beans for the upcoming dinner meal on the 12th of December.

The installation of gas and burners under steel stands (circa 1970) for the cooking pots made life a lot simpler because there was no longer a need to maintain fire for coals outside all night long. The elimination of the live coals also eliminated the carbon monoxide build-up inside La Casa de Comida. Workers before that period, including me, would have to go outside periodically to get fresh air, as the carbon monoxide would give you a severe headache.

A few years later they installed a gas heater for the building. It had been a long standing practice to precook the cut up beef the night of the eleventh and place them in two large washtubs (tinas) and let them sit covered with aluminum foil on the cold floor until the morning of the twelfth, when they would then be placed in the large cast iron pot after the chile colorado had been cooking for a while. If you put the meat in at the same time as the chile it would be overcooked and falling apart when served.

The first year the heater was installed, they left the heat on all night so the workers would be warm in the kitchen when they arrived. Picture my surprise upon arriving in the kitchen at 5 a.m. and finding the meat in the tinas boiling while sitting on the cold concrete floor, a cook's nightmare at its worst: spoiled meat. Instead of a cold kitchen, the warmth from the heater was enough to spoil the precooked meat. A quick phone call to the Pablo Fierro's explained the nightmare to them, and they came through with enough beef to prepare the chile colorado, with no time to spare.

We used 120-150 pounds of cubed beef for the chile colorado and about 250 pounds of ground beef for the albondigas.

Making the albondigas (little meat balls) is a community affair, where 30 or more members of the corporation, along with friends and relatives, show up at La Casa de Comida at 4-5 p.m. of the 11th of December to roll albondigas.

Half of the tables in the dining hall are filled with sheet metal trays of albondigas. They have to be small and of uniform size so they cook through at the same time; large ones tend to fall apart into mush. Size is so important that some of the female senior members will use their finger to flatten those not rolled right, and they have to be re-rolled to the correct size.

Everyone always wants to know what spices are in the meat balls; spices as I remember, 40 years ago, used to be brought from California by Mary Dominguez, already mixed.

The traditional spices are still used, but the mixture is still a corporation secret.

Frank Martinez scoops up albondigas from the huge pot.

Meanwhile, a large cast iron pot is kept full of boiling water and the scrap beef bones. The largest pot in the kitchen is used to simmer and cook the meat balls. The boiling hot water, without the bones, is poured into the albondigas pot containing sautéed onions. Once the big pot is at a rolling boil, a line of helpers passes the trays of meat balls to one or two people who are gently placing them into the boiling water.

A large mixing stick is used to lightly move them around to prevent them from sticking together. As the new meat balls are added, the process cools the large pot down.

More boiling water is again added from the smaller pot until the rolling boiling returns. More albondigas are added, until the last albondigas are in the pot. The gas fire is turned down to very low heat (high heat will boil the balls apart to mush), then the pot is covered to cook all night. The first thing the cooks check in the morning – did the albondigas survive the night?

Early on there were not enough large pots, space or places to cook all the pinto beans and macaroni that were needed for the dinner. Some of these were cooked at home and brought to the kitchen before the meals were served. For years Happy Apodaca would bring a mid-sized aluminum pot of beans in the morning and would sit next to the fireplace, talk, and drink coffee, until his pot was empty and washed. More stoves were added in the kitchen in the 1980s or 90s, so that all cooking is now done in the kitchen.

In my early years in the kitchen (mid-1960s), all meals were served on china, but the small water heater could not keep up with the demand. Only two small sinks presented another problem, so we washed dishes until 7-8 p.m. after the noon meal. A short time later, they installed a new sink arrangement where it is today and a larger hot water heater.

Until the beginning of the 21st century, ingredients were measured by a handful of this and a touch of that for the various items cooked. After I left David Fierro sort of inherited the main kitchen duties. He pulled Chala Fierro, his mother, aside and made physical measurements for all the food prepared to be able to recreate the recipes.

The corporation "Nuestra Senora de Guadalupe" feeds everyone who comes to the door of la Casa de Comida until the food runs out. The meal is free, the company and atmosphere are wonderful, and donations are always appreciated.

– Patrick H. Beckett

Invited guests share devotion to the Virgin of Guadalupe and dance in Her honor

Members of the Danza Azteca Chichimeca (below) and the Danza Guadalupana Azteca (right) groups perform Matachine dances that originated in Mexico's interior and were introduced to area residents. They begin dancing on the afternoon of December 11 in Tortugas.

Each year, these participants dance near the Sanctuario throughout the fiesta, then join the Tortugas Los Indios and Los Danzantes in front of the church. All attend a Mass and participate in the processions that return the palaguin to Her home in the church and to La Capilla on January 1.

Sunlight illuminates Pauline Pacheco (left) as she dances before the Sanctuario.

Above, Don Parra, the Monarca in 2013, leads dancers in the processions and performances throughout the fiesta.

Danza Azteca Chichimeca honors its heritage

Above, David Reta and Benita Pacheco participate in an abbreviated dance for the Virgin in front of the Santuario. Leonardo "Lalo" Pachecho oversees his group in 2005 on the facing page.

Laughter and tears, along with quiet reverence, permeate the conversation around the kitchen table as the founding family of Danza Azteca Chichimeca talks about the person who is no longer there – Leonardo "Lalo" Pacheco. "To me, it's been an honor to have been with this tradition, these dancers, for 64 years. I worked with my husband," says his widow, Estella, who danced with Tortugas Pueblo's Los Indios before she married. "I can do my promise in this way."

She is joined by daughters Paulina, Benita, Dorothy, Vayola, Yolanda, Eva, and Rachel, while two others, Patsy and Mary, live in California; two have died, Jessie and Jenny, as has the sole son, Leo, in the family of 12 children.

"Each of us can do something, but all of us together can only accomplish what just my mom and dad used to do," Eva observes.

"Growing up, my brother was the one who was going to lead us," adds Vayola. "All our lives were turned upside down. A lot of the men from the Danza asked what was going to happen, and my father said, 'The girls will take over'." Dorothy nods, "My dad knew it belonged in the family."

Carrying on the traditions as women remains a challenge for the family, but their dedication and desire to follow teachings of their father and grandfather, Juan Pacheco, have kept the group intact.

Around 50 members — their children, cousins, and people in the community — honor the patron saint of Mexico through dance, performing involved routines lasting up to 45 minutes during the Feast of Our Lady of Guadalupe each December 11th and 12th.

About half that number return on January 1st to join the other three Danzas, to dance, to pray, and to escort Her image back to the little Capilla.

"My grandpa immigrated into this area in 1907," Yolanda explains. "He came to the Mesquite area and south of Mesilla Park, where he would go to people's homes and be invited to dance. We have a photo dated 1914 of him with the Danza.

"My grandfather had land here and also used to graze his goats on Tortugas Mountain, and my grandmother, Sovadora, would make goat cheese they would trade for goods from the Mescalero Apaches at an arranged spot in the Organ Mountains."

The family is proud to recognize its 100th year of the group's dancing in the region and marked the anniversary with a mass and celebration in July of 2014.

Adhering to the Danza rituals, the sisters make their own costumes and spend a great deal of time considering meanings of the colors and decorations when designing their individual headdresses.

Images of the Virgin of Guadalupe cover their faces, and their skirt, called the nawia, is adorned with rows of small pieces of bamboo or reeds (carrizos) that rustle and sway with their movements, timed to the beat of the drums, all crafted by their father from deer hide and cottonwood trunks.

"Our tradition and culture is Mexican Indian, but my dad would connect with many Native American tribes. We built sweat lodges and Peace and Dignity members have gathered here. They were always welcome, and we always fed them," observes Eva.

These heirs to the Danza, which begins practice every November, invite others in the community to join in this form of prayer. "We also show patience and help the dancers who have difficulties learning," adds Dorothy.

"Our kitchen is small, but the pots grow," laughs Benita, designated the official cook in the family. The family explains the custom of moving all of the furniture

Leonardo "Lalo" Pacheco

out of the house and covering it with tarps so that the home built by Leonardo can accommodate all of the dancers and visitors. "We paid for everything."

She speaks of an "angel" who visited her kitchen one year and asked for several plates of food, and in the back of her head, she could hear her father say, "You don't deny them." Benita says, "I know it's an honor to feed people."

"We didn't have riches, but we have our culture," concludes Rachel, who smiles as her three-year-old son Anthony beats a drum nearby. "His first words were 'Da Da,' as he pointed to a picture of my father."

Pauline nods and says, "We have all experienced his presence since his death."

"It's been a journey," they all agree.

Danza Guadalupana Azteca – "It's something to rejoice about"

Danza Guadalupana Azteca members dance well into the night during the Feast of Our Lady of Guadalupe on December 12, 2014.

On the facing page, Johnny Flores plays the violin while Johnny Montoya and Rumaldo Paz, seated, watch their dancers.

Juan B. Montoya, 101, participates in the Mass marking the 100-year anniversary of the Sanctuario in 2014. He is joined by daughter Pauline Acosta and his son, Michael.

In another Tortugas adobe home, also made "brick by brick" as the family grew, Juan Montoya, 101, sits with sons Johnny, Michael, and Margarito.

He talks of his long life in the community of San Juan de Dios, already established before the Corporation claimed its 40 acres to the south, and discloses, "They were Indians and didn't have houses. They lived in jacales back then" — a fact confirmed by many residents in the Pueblo.

Montoya squints and peers into the past, envisioning a small church near Eugenio and Tortugas streets and also a nearby cemetery where his aunt was buried, a parcel now covered with homes. The Rio Grande curled through this part of the Mesilla Valley before it was tamed for irrigation, and the turtles that were so plentiful in and around the small lake to the west seemed to disappear overnight.

He lives on San Francisco Street, the dividing line between San Juan and Guadalupe and has danced for la Virgen de Guadalupe most of his life.

"I used to dance with the Indios for a few years," Montoya says. "I knew Faustino Pedraza and Pedro Pedraza."

That was before he and his sons joined with the Pacheco family's group, now known as Danza Chichimeca Azteca.

In 1967, however, the Montoyas and some other dancers decided to establish their own group and enlisted the help of a violinist from Mexico, Antonio Villareal, who shared his native Matachine dance with them.

"Our sonas come from Mexico, and our steps are different," says Johnny Montoya. Both Azteca Danzas do include the "abuelo" character, who provides comic relief and aids in the storytelling, This is common for many variations of the Matachine style, although the Pueblo Danzantes no longer enlist the clown-like figure or the toro (bull), also a part of some dances.

Photo by Jose Luis Nevarez

Their dress is similar to, but different from Danza Chichimeca Azteca's garb. And women dance in both groups, something that was uncommon in the early years of Tortugas. When asked if the costume's style has any special meaning, Michael, who drums for the group, said, "Not really. My wife is Native American, and I have borrowed some of those elements."

The headdresses resemble those of Plains Indians, and the principle color worn has ranged from yellow, to green and blue. They did retain the rows of bamboo pieces and bells that rustle and jingle to the beat of the drum. Instead of wearing the nawia, the skirt-like garment has been converted into pants.

Sadly, they relied on a recording of their violin music in 2014, after Johnny Flores was no longer able to play. The group hopes to get the recordings transcribed with the help of Danzante violinist Leo Perez and find a replacement to accompany their drum.

Juan Montoya gestures to the kitchen doorway leading into another room. "You can still see the nails where I used to hang the costumes to repair them," he says. After dancing at the baseball field and in front of the church on December 11 and 12, their delicate decorations are battered and lost. "Yes, he'd sit here for hours fixing them," Johnny nods. He says they have a "few favorite places" along ditch banks where they still gather the smaller stalks of wild bamboo.

Two of Juan's sons, four grandchildren, a great grandson, cousins, nephews, and nieces carry on this tradition and make up about one-half of the dance group. They value their heritage and look forward to performing their repertoire of 10 dances, some lasting longer than an hour.

"It's a happy occasion! It's something to rejoice about, and the community needs to be involved," Michael points out. "It's the heart of Tortugas, and if we don't do this, it won't be there for our kids and grand kids."

December 12: The Virgin's Day

Mayordomos often greet this special day with mixed feelings: Elation and satisfaction of a job well done mingle with exhaustion and sadness as the Fiesta draws to a close.

For them, December 12 begins before sunrise when they rush to the Casa de Comida to check on preparations for the enormous feast they host. The long, narrow dining room will fill and empty many times to accommodate the hundreds invited to share the noon meal.

These Fiesta sponsors coordinate tasks carried out by dozens of members "who seem to miraculously show up when you need them," says Katie Chavez.

After Capitánes paint their faces, Danzantes and Los Indios gather at the Casa del Pueblo and walk in procession to the Sanctuario, where Mayordomos join the dancers.

Current Mayordomos and those who will assume the position the next year, hold hands and pray, thanking the Virgin "for all She has done and ask that She continue to bless us," says Arianna Fierro. "It is a very humbling experience."

Danzante Eric Fierro turns to rejoin his group after paying respects to the Virgin of Guadalupe. Mayordomo Francis Wood is pictured at right.

12 observance, since I have been participating (for 48 years), is 'La Entrada' in front of the church. The church seems to stand tall against the sky," comments Francis Butler-Wood, a former Mayordoma and accomplished bailadora with Los Indios. "Somehow a hawk or two seem to know and bless us with their grace and presence. I am very fortunate to be a part of this Pueblo. I am thankful for my ancestors in my heart!"

By 9 this morning, the Mayordomos are seated at the front of the Sanctuario for Mass. They will take part in a ceremony to symbolically hand over their responsibilities to their relevos, the Pueblo members who will relieve them of their duties in the coming year.

Each one of the four current Mayordomos stepss forward, receives a lit candle, and then lights the candle of his or her replacement. After a brief blessing by the Bishop, they return to their pews, with this year's Fiesta sponsors now sitting behind the new ones.

It is an emotional event, as so is another ritual installation of new Mayordomos held in front of La Casa del Pueblo

The day's opening Entrada, when all four of the dance groups that will honor The Virgin of Guadalupe enter the large plaza in front of the church, has begun. Capitánes, singers, and drummers beating the venerated Tombe that is "the voice of the Pueblo" lead this grand entrance; all participants follow the officials and line of Indios dancers as they approach the church with small steps in time to the ancient chant.

"The most moving and solemn part of the December that is yet to come. Tears are brushed aside, hugs are shared, and couples clutch each other's hands, but the full day ahead quickly diverts their attention.

Dancing continues all morning, with Los Danzantes and Los Indios taking turns directly in front of the church — and the altar and image of the Virgin of Guadalupe inside. Visitors are gently reminded by Capitánes to avoid standing as a barrier between the dance and its intended beneficiary.

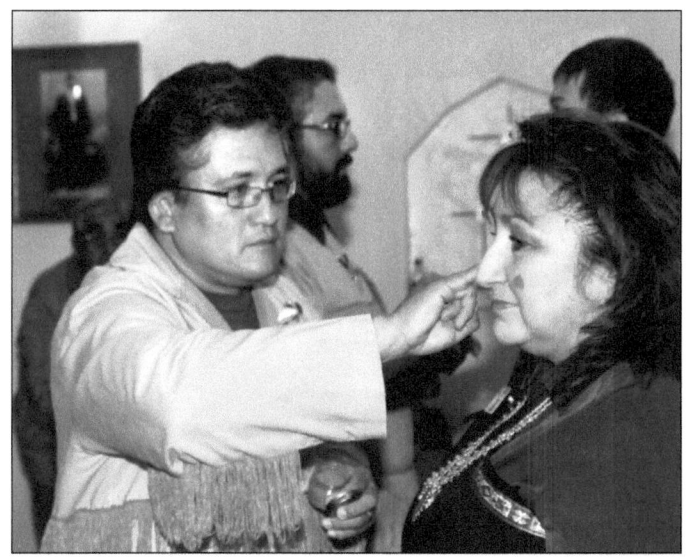

Capitán Miguel Parra paints the face of Rosie Stewart in La Capilla before the day's events begin in 2014.

La Entrada brings all four dance groups together in front of the Sanctuario de Nuestra Señora during the morning of December 12. Capitánes in this 1997 image include Joseph Loera, Ralph Paz, David Ferrales, and Robert Parra. Los Indios, Fiesta officials and Los Danzantes, Danza Azteca Chichimeca, and Danza Guadalupana Azreca dance to Pueblo chants and the beat of the Tombé, played by Pablo Fierro.

Photos (2) by Jose Luis Nevarez

Bishop Emeritus Ricardo Ramirez

Violin, then drumming and song guide the dancers who move with precision and grace. Vivid ribbons catch the light and take flight with each turn. Little Malinches and the crowned Monarca weave through Danzantes, whose cupiles radiate the image of the Virgin.

The drums and chants take on a life of their own at times. "When we dance, I always want my dad to sing — the songs are a whole different thing," says Junshiro Molinar. He has to adjust his dance to the different variation, which is something inexperienced dancers find challenging.

"I sometimes play the drum and not know what it's going to be," observes David Fierro. "But experienced dancers know what to do. It was almost like Emma (Narvaez) was directing the drum."

The two Azteca groups dance throughout the day as well. Danza Guadalupana Azteca sets up its altar to the Virgin at the baseball field east of the church, where they also performed the previous afternoon.

Danza Chichimeca Azteca's altar is constructed on the north side of the church plaza, where an oversized portrait of the Virgen de Guadalupe, surrounded by flowers and candles, blesses the dancers.

> "Is the name Guadalupe Spanish? No! Is it English? No! It's Arabic and means the 'River of Life.'
>
> "Today you're going to dance for the blessed Virgin Mary — that's a very good thing. La Virgen is very close to God, and that's why we ask her to pray for us."
>
> — Bishop Ricardo Ramirez

This is the third day of their performance, as they also honor Juan Diego on December 10. But members of both groups do not reveal the tiredness that invades their muscles. "The dances are not easy. Because it's so physical, it takes every ounce of our mind, body, and spirit," says Eva Pacheco. Her sister Vayola adds, "It's like we leave this world."

Around noon, the Danzantes, Indios, and Pueblo leaders walk in procession to the west side of the Casa de Comida, where the aroma of albondigas and chile escapes the building that has undergone more than one expansion since it was constructed as early as 1916.

Los Indios and Los Danzantes form a large circle and invite onlookers to join a dance, La Rueda, that encompasses the large lot. Drummers and singers travel the interior of the circle, ramping up the beat in an enthusiastic and joyful song that invigorates the crowd.

The meal is free, but donations are appreciated. "I actually did try to count how many we served," recalls Rosemary Kirby, "but I gave up when I got to 1,200!"

Photo by Jose Luis Nevarez

Most Rev. Ricardo Ramirez, Bishop Emeritus, conducts the installation of new Mayordomos ceremony during the December 12 Mass.

At left, new Mayordomos for 2015 (left) William Martinez and Lorraine Padilla light their candles from those held by 2014 Mayordomos (from front) Bill Acosta, Libby Valles, Christine Misquez and Lawrence Jimenez. Not shown are J.R. and Rosie Stewart. The ceremony usually attracts a standing-room-only crowd.

Photo by Jose Luis Nevarez

Danza Chichimeca Azteca places an altar with a large portrait of Nuestra Señora de Guadalupe where the group dances just north of the church (top left).

Above, Rumaldo Paz, Jr. (Mister) plays for Los Indios during the 12th of December celebration.

Danzante members each create their own distinctive cupiles.

Although the faces change throughout the years, the traditions remain. Pictured above are Ritchie Rosales and Rosie Stewart.

At right, Emma Narvaez well into her 70s, dances one last year. Barbara Frietze joins her.

Three times the children of Freddie Martinez faced life-threatening health issues, and three times their father made promises to the Virgin of Guadalupe.

After praying, he assured his wife that the children would recover; Martinez never broke his vows to honor Her in Tortugas.

Those children still travel from California each year to honor their father's wishes. "Where else would we be?" asks daughter Jeannie Drennan.

His grandchildren wrote to him in 1999: "For the past 50 years the Virgin continues to help and bless us. As for the rest of the family, we sit in awe of such a dedicated and faithful man. We, too, go to the Virgin because of you."

The Feast: All are welcome

Mayordomos Reymundo Molinar and Rosemary Kirby take part in 2010's La Rueda, the circle dance, that everyone is encouraged to join. Pablo Fierro sings the chant that accompanies this dance with fellow drummers and singers that rotate within the circle's interior. Dancers and Pueblo officials will then enter the Casa de Comida for the first serving of the popular noon meal.

Dancers are invited in to eat, served first at the long tables. Bowls of steaming albondigas — the cook did a good job last night — and red chile meat and beans are passed, while volunteers scoop up bowls to be refilled and cups that need more coffee or cocoa. The rich macaroni and cheese and thick slices of Indian bread also quickly disappear.

Before heading back out to dance for the afternoon, members snatch a handful of biscochos, homemade at the Pueblo earlier that week.

All are invited to eat during this feast, and the line of hungry people snakes around the side of the building and spills into a nearby parking lot. Once one group finishes its meal, the tables are cleaned and reset, and another group takes its place until the food runs out or workers need to close the kitchen to prepare for another event that evening.

"Mayordomos used to have to pay for the meals, the biscochos, everything, themselves," remembers Pablo Fierro, who served as a Mayordomo eight times. "We would try to get donations of a calf if we could because the meat is so expensive."

Now, they still rely heavily on donations and must remain within a certain budget provided by the Corporation. As food costs rise, feeding all who wish to eat becomes more of a challenge.

Top right, Bertha Tellez (right) and Jane Hernandez line up to refill bowls of albondigas in 2005. Cooks are busy throughout the day, when hundreds fill the Pueblo dining hall during the feast day.

With barely enough room to maneuver, servers replace empty bowls of chile colorado, albondigas, and frijoles for the hungry crowd that descends on La Casa de Comida.

Emma Narvaez was often in charge of the dessert table for the enchilada dinners. In the 1991 image above, she offers sweets in La Casa de Comida. Her son, Henry, helps as they stand in front of an historical photo that features Emma dancing as a young Malinche at the front of the maypole.

At right, Rosemary Herrera Aquilar delivers bread in 2014, with the help of Evelyn Herrera Castillo.

Facing page: Los Danzantes dance before the church, where the image of the Virgin resides on December 12.

The afternoon reverberates with different drum beats, violin melodies, and chanting. The energy remains high as dancers achieve their purpose of honoring La Virgen on Her day. The sounds, the swirl of color, the movement become hypnotic.

Late afternoon, Mayordomos grasp the handles of the palanguin inside the church and escort the image in a procession that slowly advances to the Casa del Pueblo. Dancing to their own accompaniment, the groups approach the image, bow, and return to their position behind the other dancers. Corporation and parish members trail behind the Mayordomos with the choir to sing hymns that praise the Virgin of Guadalupe. A gilded radiance tints the scene as the sun drops to the horizon — another blessing bestowed on this December 12.

At a line that is drawn directly in front of the Casa del Pueblo, there is the second ceremony that recognizes the new Mayordomos, who once again switch positions with the ones who sponsored this fiesta. Los Indios honor the new sponsors with a dance, then join the others in a procession that takes the image back to the church, where She will stay until the New Year. A rosary follows, and after the service Pueblo members are treated to a reception hosted by the new Mayordomos in the Casa de Comida.

Danzantes pile their cupiles on cars outside to air. They are free from confinement until they, along with Los Indios, conclude their final dances for the day in the Casa del Pueblo.

Appreciation, announcements, and apologies are expressed in the meeting house, and after a final hand shake, touch on the shoulder, or promise to see each other soon, these devotees of La Virgen disperse into the winter night ... knowing they will return on New Year's Day, to begin the cycle once more.

"Mine is the family of Jimmy Herrera. My father danced for 42 years, my brother Paul danced for 32 years, and myself — 30 years! I enjoy being a part of the Corporation, and I'll forever remember when the Danzantes dance all night. The bonfire is also a great celebration for me and all of my family."   — Joe Herrera

"I started dancing with the Indios December 1980. My grandpa Ernesto Dominquez and grandma Elvira Dominquez taught me to dance. 2009 was a special year. I was Mayordoma with my dad and mom, Daniel Flores and Lupe Dominquez Flores, and my cousin, Arturo Montoya."   — Sylvia R. Kreager

"I can tell you one thing for sure - the Fiesta wouldn't happen without the Fierros. Look who's always working behind the scenes."   —Martín Barela

"At an early age of 5 years old, I began dancing with the Danzantes as a Malinche with my sister Jesusita (Jessie) Herrera, under the direction of Pino Moreno, then Monarca and later it was Isidro Fierro as the Monarca. I danced with them until I was 13 years of age, then I was transferred to the Grupo De Indias until I was 20 years of age. Also at this age, I became a Mayordoma, due to unforeseen circumstances. I filled in for my sister Jesusita.   — Manuela (Nellie) Herrera Bustillos

Junshiro Molinar dances to the Tombé and chants of (from left) Francisco Rayos, Frank Villegas, Ralph and Phillip Paz during the December 12 observance.

Below, Danzantes honor the Virgin on Her day while violinist Leo Perez plays the age-old melodies for the Matachine group of the Pueblo. Pictured from front are Paul Herrera, Lawrence Jimenez, and Mike Marta.

On the facing page, Bianca Paz performs Los Indios dances, whose steps she learned from her family.

Sally and Ray Hernandez, Bobby Parra, Jr., and Felicia Parra take the image of the Virgin of Guadalupe from the Sanctuario for the late-afternoon procession.

"We used to come home from school and cry, 'Why do we have to be Indians' after the kids called us names. My mom used to tell us, 'Never be ashamed of what we are and be strong. Don't forget who you are and what your mama has taught you — to believe and have pride in what we are. Believe in our culture, and believe in our sacred prayers.'"
— Fermina Paz

"I've been blessed with a wonderful family, and I attribute this to being devoted to the Virgin. When I need help, I can rely on Her. We get a feeling of satisfaction by helping those people who make a vow to La Virgen. We feel we've got something; we are able to help them."
— Pablo Fierro

Los Indios begin their dance to approach the Virgin's image during the 2009 procession.

Los Danzantes honor Her in the 2012 Fiesta (below).

Nuestra Señora blesses Tortugas during Procession

Bailadoras with Los Indios take turns bowing before the image of Our Lady of Guadalupe while Mayordomos and Pueblo members slowly take Her image through the village of Tortugas. She is escorted from the church to the Casa del Pueblo where new Mayordomos will assume their responsibilities as Fiesta sponsors for 2015. From left, Libby Valles, Henry Narvaez, Bill Acosta, Arturo Montoya, Reymundo Molinar, Rosie Stewart, Lawrence Jimenez, and Christine Misquez escort the Virgin on her journey around the village.

"The procession in the afternoon on the 12th symbolizes everything that we are about in our cultural and our basic beliefs about life and the afterlife.

There are three parts: the traveling, the arriving, and the new beginning. The journey is just as important as the destination. We recognize that life is a journey and there are ups and downs, happiness and sadness.

The arrival is two parts: You're glad to be there and sad to be leaving. The arrival is just as important as the journey.

After the arrival there's a new beginning celebrated with a different canto; we dedicate the new journey with a canto — and then we start our new journey. "
　　　　　　　　　　　　　　　　— Henry Narvaez

Los Danzantes members retreat to the back of the dancers' line after paying respects to the image of the Virgin as the Indios approach in this 2013 procession.

Below, Mayordomos Mary Lou and Antonio Marta, left, carry the image with Joe and La Donna Loera in 1997.

Photo by Jose Luis Nevarez

Above, Mayordomos turn "their" Virgin over to their replacements in an emotional ceremony. Pictured above in 1991 are Rev. Giles Carie, O.F.M. Conv., Ralph Paz, Fred and Marta Salas, Margarito (Maggie) Fierro (making the transfer) and Reymundo and Delores Molinar.

A young Danza Guadalupana Azteca member, top right, happily races through the streets during the procession around the village.

Indios recognize the new Mayordomos (left) Antonio Avalos, Jason Jones, and Arianna Fierro. Daniel Flores and Sylvia R. Kreager stand behind, after turning the image over to the new Mayordomos in 2009 (facing page).

← *Tortugas at 100* ⫷

Danza Guadalupana Azteca dancers join the procession around Tortugas in 2013 (top, facing page).

Vayola and Crystal Pacheco, Danza Azteca Chicimeca members, take a turn carrying the sacred image on the return trip to the Sanctuario (facing page).

Crowds surround La Virgen as Mayordomos escort Her through the village in the late afternoon light (above).

"We don't have material wealth in Tortugas — we don't allow commercialism. Our traditions make us rich."
— David Fierro

"My grandmother, Francisca Roybal, was the only woman Indian chief in Tortugas. Before we were Christianized, my ancestors believed in the elements. I fear the rituals are being done away with, but the Virgin is up there. She'll know what to do."
— Emma Narvaez

Rev. Vincent Peterson waits outside the Sanctuario de Nuestra Señora de Guadalupe on December 12 after the image has been taken to the church, where the faithful may visit Her until January 1.

(Top) Cupiles worn by Danzantes air at the end of the Fiesta.

Rey Molinar, Jr., Henry Narvaez. amd Miguel Parra chant on the way back to the Casa del Pueblo.

The Next 100 Years ...

Photo by Jose Luis Nevarez

Rain, snow, and a bitter wind accompany dancers during La Entrada in 2015. Capitánes Bill Acosta, Mike Marta, Miguel Parra (Capitán de la Guerra), Reymundo Molinar, and Michael Molinar lead the dancers to the church.

Significant changes and also the fear of losing their tribal lands have already challenged Los Indigenes de Nuestra Señora de Guadalupe just two years into the Pueblo's second century of existence.

More Tortugas elders, beloved family members, Fiesta participants and supporters have seen their last Día Doce, at least from this earthly perspective. Their presence is missed, yet their spirit infuses their successors with perseverance and grace.

Fiesta Sponsors Invite All Dancers in 2015

For the traditional Feast on December 12, the Mayordomos, William Martinez, Lorraine Padilla, and Rosie and Juan R. Stewart invited the Danza Guadalupana Azteca and Danza Azteca Chichimeca to La Casa de Comida.

Volunteers bustled among the tables filled with colorful dancers during the first seating. In past years these Matachine dance groups broke for lunch at the Pacheco home or the parish hall.

Fiesta sponsors for 2016, Diane Gomez, along with Ralph, Kathy and Phillip Paz, extended the invitation for the upcoming celebration in 2016 as well.

134   ←   *Tortugas at 100*   ⤛

Following in his father's footsteps, the new Cacique, Patrick Narvaez, is determined to carry his ancestors' traditions further into the 21st Century. Patrick served a probationary period before being formally recognized as the current spiritual leader by La Corporación in 2016.

The Cacique's Path

A familiar, high-pitched screeeee echoes from deep arroyos and announces the hawk, before it can be seen. Drifting on Tortugas Mountain thermals, its presence is expected — and welcome — as a small cluster of people watch the graceful bird soar skyward, then disappear.

"Nobody wants to leave," whispers Lupe Dominquez Flores, as she closes her eyes and faces the slight breeze that cools moist skin this late summer morning. "It's so peaceful here," says another Pueblo member.

"Sacred," someone else offers, looking across the desert landscape and patchwork of farmland that hugs the Rio Grande, which brought the antepasados, their ancestors, to the Mesilla Valley.

The person being honored this day, Patrick Narvaez, is the newly selected Cacique (spiritual leader), and he traces his roots to these early days more than a century ago. For all of his 39 years, he remembers learning Native American rituals and chants from his grandmother, Emma Narvaez, and father, Henry, who at 70 officially turns his position over to his son in a ceremony atop the desert peak.

Temperatures climb along with the elevation, and a refreshing detour through New Mexico State University sprinklers on the way becomes a memory. The trek is challenging during the winter pilgrimage on December 11, but brutal as sun breaks through occasional clouds this August day in 2015.

While taking a break in the scant shade of a mesquite tree, Henry recounts one perilous trip many Pueblo members still recall: "My mother was not yet 10, and it was snowing pretty hard. The Cacique determined that it was too dangerous for the women to accompany male Corporation members and pilgrims. Well, their reaction was: 'We're not doing this because of Francisco Dominquez. We made a promise to la Virgen!'

Henry Narvaez speaks of past journeys to Tortugas Mountain before climbing the peak with his son, Patrick.

Pueblo officials gather at the top of Tortugas Mountain after a ceremony welcomes the new Cacique of Tortugas Pueblo. From left: Arturo Montoya, Henry Narvaez, Michael Molinar, Miguel Parra, Patrick Narvaez, and Bill Acosta.

"Men and women all made it up the mountain and celebrated Mass. When they came down, the conditions were miserable, and they knew they were in trouble.

"The snow was blinding. They ended up following the wrong arroyo on the way back to Tortugas and were eventually found — wandering near Mesquite," far to the south of their destination," Henry Narvaez says. He adds, "There are several other stories we don't share; they have to do with the supernatural."

As the handful of people ascend the mountain, progress slows, with frequent breaks to rest and survey the rocky and cactus-filled surroundings. One desert plant, the sotol, is harvested to make walking sticks (quiotes) for the December pilgrimage; it spears the sky with elongated blooms that buzz with bees. "We used to gather the sotol right here from the mountain, but we almost wiped it out," Henry Narvaez explains. "I'm glad to see it's recovered."

The walkers reach the summit where Humero Michael Molinar and Capitán de la Guerra Miguel Parra, several other Corporación members, along with residents of Tortugas await. They quietly watch as Henry blesses Patrick and passes his staff to his

son."Gracias — a Dios, La Virgen y todos," Parra says when asked to speak.

Molinar reminds the group that all must work together in order to retain Pueblo customs. "It takes everybody; we're all here for a reason. We do what we have to do for the good of the Pueblo, mankind, and Mother Earth. That's what is sacred and what we pray for. Hopefully, at the end of our time, we learn a bit of gratitude for our ancestors," he says.

After witnessing his father serve as chief, Patrick, who admits he couldn't sleep the previous night, realizes that his new position demands both sacrifice and a deep reverence for tradition.

"Our antepasados would be proud of us," he tells the gathering. "But it breaks my heart to look out here and see all of these houses. We've got to make sure we are still able to come up here for the next 100 years. We must instill this heritage in our children; otherwise, we'll lose it."

While others linger on the mountain, the new Cacique picks his way down Tortugas Mountain and walks back to the village, this time with the Humero. His father watches as the walkers shrink in the distance, knowing their journey will continue.

Concern for Tortugas Mountain Resurfaces

As 2015 and 2016 propel the Pueblo into its future, plans are being considered for a dense development, "Aggie Uptown," east of New Mexico State University to the base of Tortugas Mountain.

The university proposes a partnership with private entities to create a mix of commercial development, a new golf course, medical offices, assisted living space, residential areas, and expansion of NMSU program space. North-south arterials could extend into the area as early as 2017, with the possible addition of another freeway exit south of University Avenue, which will block access to the sacred peak during the annual pilgrimage.

"That is something that will definitely affect us in the next 100 years," says Dominic Fierro.

New Mexico State University graduate student Kate Moore has been working with the Pueblo for the past two years to protect the trails that have led the faithful up Tortugas Mountain for generations. With a National Register of Historic Places designation, it is hoped the mountain itself will be better protected.

Rosemary Kirby cites Native American scholar and sociologist Phillip de Loria when she says: "Our nation does not hesitate to trample on sacred ground. Many times, the reasons are simply for commercial value. Should/when the busy outside world of NMSU or of Las Cruces continues to infringe on centuries-old traditions of Tortugas Pueblo and its people, their actions will impact our actions, but not stop them."

Photo by Jose Luis Nevarez

Danzantes and the faithful escort the Virgin's image, surrounded by 2015 and 2016 Mayordomos, from the Casa del Pueblo to the Sanctuario de Nuestra Señora de Guadalupe before dawn on December 11.

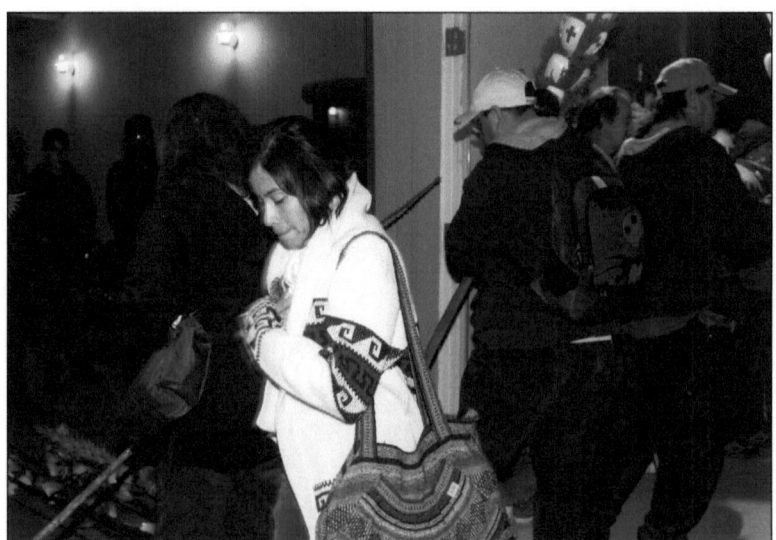

Upon returning to the Casa del Pueblo on December 11, pilgrims give thanks for a successful journey.

Piro-Manso-Tiwa Tribe Challenges Tortugas Claim to Pueblo Land/Artifacts — Again

A dispute from Los Indigenes de Nuestra Señora de Guadalupe's past has once again cast a shadow on Tortugas and its heritage. Elders have often mentioned a splinter group, which identifies itself as Piro-Manso-Tiwa Tribe of the Pueblo of San Juan de Guadalupe — usually not in a positive way. According to Corporation minutes, interviews and a document written by Emma Narvaez, who knew those involved and whose grandmother was Francisca Roybal, Cacica Regenta in 1914, La Corporación voted to select a new President in 1947.

The members replaced Victor Roybal, Sr., who had moved to California and was said to have made disturbing decisions concerning Tortugas ancestral items and land, illegally selling it or transferring it to family members and losing possession of La Casa de Comida because of unpaid property taxes.

Records show newly elected officers were: Miguel Fierro, President; Ernesto Dominguez, Vice President; Felipe Carabajal, Treasurer; and Emma Narvaez, Secretary.

Elders also recounted that President Roybal returned to Tortugas only on December 11 each year, when he would collect for himself the donations that funded the Fiesta. After a series of court battles from 1948-58, Roybal was ordered to return the Pueblo's sacred possessions, and title of property was transferred to its rightful owner since 1914, La Corporación.

Members of the PMT group have been trying unsuccessfully to attain federal recognition as a Native American Pueblo since 1973 and in 2015 submitted another petition, which insulted Tortugas Pueblo and claimed some time-honored Tortugas traditions as its own. PMT Cacique Edward Roybal also appeared before the Las Cruces City Council and Doña Ana County Commission in March of 2016 to seek letters of support from the local governing bodies.

Los Indigenes President Arianna Fierro spoke eloquently during the meetings about how approval of the PMT application could be devastating for Tortugas.

"Our position on this matter has not changed. There are no assurances that if they were to obtain federal recognition that they would not seek to disenfranchise La Corporación and displace the community of Tortugas," she said. "And you should be aware it's not only the real estate that they claim as theirs, but our historical artifacts as well."

The city council decided to table the request for an unspecified time and did not submit a letter. County commissioners, however, voted 3-2 in favor of supporting the PMT designation.

Dozens of Los Indios members and Tortugas residents attended the sessions. Once again, Tortugas Pueblo prepared and sent a document to the U.S. Department of the Interior asking that the petition be denied. The Piro-Manso-Tiwa Tribe of the Pueblo of San Juan de Guadalupe awaits a decision – and so do Los Indigenes de Nuestra Señora de Guadalupe.

What the Future Holds

"I think the future is uncertain, but we have to stick with it — and ask for guidance from the spirits," says Michael Molinar. "This really isn't that much different than what our people faced 500 years ago, when they were displaced."

Sonia Lazos agrees; she adds, "As long as people are willing to serve, it won't ever die. But these youngsters want to go to school, work, and make better lives for themselves, as they should; and so they'll leave. It makes it harder and harder."

"The same thing is happening in other pueblos, and not to say the young ones won't come back, but here we are very, very few. The elders serve for many years," Molinar says. He quotes son Junshiro who joined the Marines in 2016: "All we can do is keep doing the work."

Iashire Molinar, who is 14, notices, "Change is in the air. But some kids my age, especially those who dance with the Matachines, are really into it."

"The future of the Fiesta and the Corporation will remain strong amid the coming changes. My certainty rests on past history and the strength of our faith in Our Lady of Guadalupe," writes Rosemary Kirby from her northern New Mexico home. "Take a look at the tremendous changes in the past century-plus years:

The Fiesta, the traditions, all have, not only survived, but incorporated all of the changes. The path for the pilgrimage changed its course, somewhat, because an interstate highway was built.

"There are many examples of the changes in the past 100 years, but the Corporation has absorbed them by adapting to them. I cannot imagine a (man-made) change that our people would not be able to overcome by use of their creative/rational/faith-full abilities.

"Look at the original Tepeyac — the Cathedral of Our Lady of Guadalupe in Mexico City is now surrounded by a very modern urban area; yet, millions of people still fill it every day, but especially during the 12th of December.

"It is faith that maintains its purpose, there and here: it is the tremendous faith of the people of Tortugas Pueblo (the Corporation) that will continue this tradition," Kirby concludes.

All speak with reverence about their life within the Pueblo. "I believe I live in the best place in the world," says David Ferrales, Jr.

"Being from Tortugas is an honor; when you can step out your door and be surrounded by these traditions, I feel that I am one of the lucky ones. And I was fortunate enough to know and dance with the elders," he reflects.

Sonia Lazos, second from left, joins Los Indios dancers (from right) Becky Rios-Chavez, Arianna Fierro, Francis Wood, Eddie Rios, Junshiro Molinar, and Anthony Parra during the 2015 Rueda.

Capitán David Fierro waits with Los Indios for his chance to visit the Virgin's image after the San Juan dances in June of 2015.

Tortugas residents decorate their homes for the fiesta; Carolina Carabajal's home is pictured below.

Fermina Paz and her son Rafael "Buddy" Paz watch dancers honoring San Juan de Bautista in 2016.

A Prayer

Creator, Great Mystery,
Let me be ever aware of the dignity
which you have graced on all Beings;
remind me of the humility
which you have bestowed upon me;
help me become worthy of this task you have handed me.

— Rosemary Estrada Kirby